The Tao of Objects

A Beginner's Guide to Object-Oriented Programming

. . . .

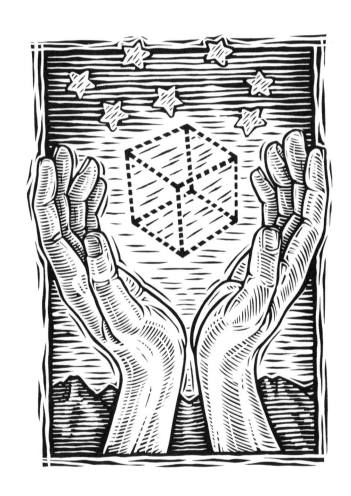

Gary Entsminger

M&T BOOKS

M&T Books
A Division of M&T Publishing, Inc.
501 Galveston Drive
Redwood City, CA 94063

Library of Congress Cataloging-in-Publication Data

Entsminger, Gary, 1950–
    The Tao of objects: a beginner's guide to object-oriented programming / Gary Entsminger
        p.   cm.
    Includes bibliographical references and index.
    ISBN 1-55851-155-5
    1. Object-oriented programming (Computer science)   I. Title.
QA76.64.E58   1990
005.1—dc20
                                                         90-22920
                                                            CIP

93 92 91 90   4   3   2   1

Project Editor: Linda Comer   **Cover Design**: Lauren Smith Designs
Cover Illustration: Christine Mortensen   **Inside Illustrations**: Mike Sagara

For Alison

Contents

WHY THIS BOOK IS FOR YOU 1

INTRODUCTION BY BRUCE ECKEL...3

CHAPTER 1: GREAT JOURNEYS, SINGLE STEPS.............................17
About the Book 18
Choose Your Language 19
Objects and Actions 21
A World of Objects 24
About Inheritance 25
Building a New Type 29
Inheritance Among OOP Languages 31
Overriding Behavior and Data 31
About Polymorphism 32
Static and Dynamic Binding 36
Dynamic Programming 38
Another View 39
Object Types 39
About Types 42
Constructors and Destructors 45
The Importance of Being Constructed 48
Messages 49

CHAPTER 2: THINKING IN OBJECTS 53
Complex Numbers 59
Operator Overloading in C++ 60
Types, Not Individuals 61

How Complex Should Objects Be? 62
Base and Abstract Types 63
Abstract vs. Concrete 67
Planning for Change..68
The Trickle-Up Theory 69
Objects, Classes, and Types 70

CHAPTER 3: EXTENDING THE SYSTEM...................................**73**
Sketching Your Objects 79
Reusing Code 80
Choosing a First Application 81
Checkers and Chess 82
Black Art..86
Chaos Theory and Strange Attractors 90
Mathematic Attraction 91
Inheriting Strange Attractors 93
Display Window 94
State Space 96
Model = State Generator 97
Where OOP Works Best 99
Extending Systems 100

CHAPTER 4: SHAPING THE SYSTEM......................................**111**
Dynamics 116
Constructors, Destructors, and Responsibility 118
Managing From the Bottom Up 119
Tracing Through Pointers 125
Some Advantages..127

CHAPTER 5: DYNAMIC STYLE **137**
Expert Systems..140
OOP in AI 142
Frames vs. Objects 142
Finding the Objects 143
Programming for Change 152

CHAPTER 6: AN OBJECT-ORIENTED NEURAL NETWORK **165**
Objects and Networks 169
Deriving New Networks 176
Data Lists and Events...177

CHAPTER 7: DESIGNING WITH OBJECTS............................**191**
An Alternative to Chaos 192
What's Wrong With This Picture? 194
Programming for Change 197
Object-Oriented System Design 199
The Five Stages of Object Design 202
More on Object Discovery 204
An Example 205
The Object-Oriented Design System 206
The Complexity Test 211
OOP and GUI 211
Libraries and Frameworks 212
Skeptic's Corner 213
The Art of Software Design 214

AFTERWORD BY ZACK URLOCKER **217**

APPENDIX A: GLOSSARY **225**

APPENDIX B: REFERENCES AND RESOURCES **237**

APPENDIX C: A CONCISE COMPARISON OF C++, TURBO PASCAL, AND SMALLTALK **243**

Acknowledgements

I'd like to thank a few folks who've supported and advised me, offered suggestions, read the manuscript, provided software, or just plain been helpful during the writing of this book: Brenda McLaughlin and Linda Comer at M&T Books; Zack Urlocker, David Intersimone, Nan Borreson, and Tammy Casey at Borland International; J.D. Hildebrand and Larry O'Brien at *Computer Language*; Mike Floyd at *Dr. Dobb's Journal*; Bill Gates at *Midnight Engineering*; and Susan Allen, Billy Barr, and Alison Brody at the Rocky Mountain Biological Laboratory.

I especially thank Bruce Eckel, Chester Anderson, and Larry Fogg for the many hours of discussions and idea exchanges while I was planning and writing. I can't wait to see what you three do next.

Small portions of this book first appeared in different form in *AI Expert*, *Computer Language*, *Dr. Dobb's Journal*, *Micro Cornucopia*, and *Neural Network News*.

The quotes by Lao-tzu from *The Tao Te Ching* are from the Stephen Mitchell translation (Harper & Row, New York, N.Y., 1988).

The quote by Douglas Hofstadter and Daniel Dennett is from *The Mind's I* (Bantam Books, New York, N.Y., 1981).

The quotes by Fritjof Capra are from *The Tao of Physics* (Shambhala, Berkeley, Calif., 1975).

The quote by Riane Eisler is from *The Chalice and the Blade* (Harper & Row, San Francisco, Calif., 1987).

The quote by David Rumelhart and James McClelland is from *Parallel Distributed Processing* (MIT Press, Cambridge, Mass., 1987).

The inside illustrations are based on photographs by Chester Anderson.

Why This Book is For You

This book can help you understand the key concepts of object-oriented programming. It's written for C and Pascal programmers who want to know how they can rethink their programs using objects.

The Tao of Objects is a friendly, hands-on book that emphasizes the key advantages of programming with objects. The examples in the book are general enough to be of interest to anyone — and they're fun.

Subjects of particular interest include:

- Object-oriented design

- Program extension

- Modeling systems

- Chaos theory and strange attractors

- Linked lists

- Expert systems

and much more. All examples are given in both C++ and Turbo Pascal, the object-oriented successors to C and Pascal.

If you're a C or Pascal programmer who wants a gentler introduction to object-oriented programming than a computer manual can provide, this book is for you.

Introduction

Expressing the ideas of object-oriented programming in terms of an Eastern philosophy is a wonderful concept. Gary and I spent many days in the woods and the mountains and many hours on the phone working on this view. Time being what it is (fleeting), I found I didn't have enough, and the book became Gary's. However, I hope I can make additional contributions in this introduction by raising some of the issues I feel are important.

When I explained OOP to my friend Mark (a psychologist), he replied "I don't understand — how else would you do it? How were they doing it before?" I found I was at a loss to describe the old way. I mean, I practiced procedural programming and all that, but it never really made sense to me — it never seemed *whole*. In fact, I never took programming that seriously before OOP, probably because it seemed to take too much effort to get the job done. Because I can now think in much more powerful terms, I can solve much more complex problems.

One difficulty people have when learning object-oriented programming is finding a way to think about it. Often you hear such unhelpful things as "It's easier for someone who doesn't know how to program to learn OOP than for an experienced programmer" or "You need to unlearn what you know." My personal experience has not supported this. Although thinking about objects is different from thinking about procedural programming, it's different because you're stepping into a larger world, not because everything you know is wrong. This is especially true with hybrid languages like C++ and Turbo Pascal; you'll see that the ability to create user-defined data types isn't such a radical idea, since you use data types so much that you usually don't even think about them. However, it does tend to highlight the limitations of the built-in types and (to my mind) the relative primitiveness of what we've been using as programming languages so far. Once you begin using an object-oriented language, it's hard to go back.

History and Concepts

When the Simula language was developed in Scandinavia in the late sixties, its designers were trying to make the process of simulation easier (hence the name). Simulations always seem to involve a group of things — customers in line in a bank, molecules of air, migrating animals — in short, a lot of objects. An object knows things about itself: It has an internal state, or characteristics. It can also do things: It has external operations, or behaviors. It turns out that this also describes the data types built into a programming language. It's just that the data types cannot express the features necessary to model a real-world system.

Existing languages engendered very messy code when a simulation was created because their types were so limited. It looked like the only way to make simulation easy was to change the language so the programmer could add new types of data. This abstract data typing is a fundamental concept in object-oriented programming. Abstract data types work almost exactly like built-in types: You can create variables of a type (called *instances* in object-oriented parlance) and manipulate those variables (called *sending messages*; you send a message and the variable figures out what to do with it).

The language designers also discovered that a type does more than describe the constraints on a set of objects; it also has a relationship with other types. Two types can have characteristics and behaviors in common, but one type may contain more characteristics than another and may also handle more messages (or handle them differently). Inheritance was developed to express this relationship between types. It uses the concept of base types and derived types. A base type has all the characteristics and behaviors that are shared among the types derived from it. You create a base type to represent the core of your ideas about the objects in your system. From it, you derive other types to express the different ways that core can be realized.

For example, a garbage-recycling machine sorts pieces of garbage. The base type is garbage, and each piece of garbage has a weight, a value, and so on and can be shredded, melted, or decomposed. From this, we derive specific types of garbage that may have additional characteristics (a bottle has a color) or behaviors (an aluminum can may be crushed, a steel can is magnetic). In addition, some behaviors may be different (the value of paper depends on its type and condition). Using inheritance, you can build a type hierarchy that expresses the problem you're trying to solve in terms of its types.

Casting the solution in the same terms as the problem is tremendously beneficial because you don't need a lot of intermediate models (used with procedural languages for large problems) to get from a description of the problem to a description of the solution (inevitably in terms of computers, in pre-object-oriented languages). The type hierarchy is the primary model, so you go directly from the description of the system in the real world to the description of the system in code. Indeed, one of the difficulties people have with object-oriented design is that it's too simple for a mind trained to look for complex ways to get from the beginning to the end. When I say "The types are the primary model, and the best representation for the types is the code," most people don't believe me (at first).

Once you've modeled your problem as a set of types, writing the code becomes remarkably simple; it's mostly a matter of creating variables and sending messages to them. The variables take care of the details and ensure their own integrity.

When dealing with type hierarchies, you often want to treat an object not as the specific type that it is but as a member of its base type. This allows you to write code that doesn't depend on specific types. For instance, the now-classic "shape" example has functions that manipulate generic shapes without respect to whether they're circles, squares, triangles, and so on. Since all shapes can be drawn, erased, and moved, these functions simply send a message to a shape object; they don't worry about how the object copes with the message.

Such code is unaffected by the addition of new types, which is the most common way to extend an object-oriented program to handle new situations. For instance, you can derive a new subtype of *shape* called *pentagon* without modifying the functions that deal only with generic shapes. The ability to extend a program easily by deriving new subtypes is important because it greatly reduces the cost of software maintenance (the so-called "software crisis" was caused by the observation that software was costing more than people thought it ought to).

There's a problem, however, with attempting to treat derived-type objects as their generic base types (circles as shapes, bicycles as vehicles, cormorants as birds). If a function is going to tell a generic shape to draw itself, or a generic vehicle to steer, or a generic bird to fly, the compiler cannot know at compile time precisely what piece of code will be executed. That's the point — when the message is sent, the programmer doesn't *want* to know what piece of code will be executed; the function can be equally applied to a circle, square, or triangle, and the object will execute the proper code depending on its specific type. If you add a new subtype, the code it executes can be different without changes to the function. Since the compiler cannot know precisely what piece of code is executed, what does it do?

The answer is the primary twist in object-oriented programming: The compiler cannot make a function call in the traditional sense. The function call generated by a non-OOP compiler causes what is called *early binding*, a term you may not have heard before because you've never thought about it any other way. It means the compiler generates a call to a specific function name, and the linker resolves that call to an absolute address of the code to be executed. In OOP, the program cannot determine the address of the code until run time, so some other scheme is necessary when a message is sent to a generic object.

To solve the problem, object-oriented languages use the concept of *late binding*. When you send a message to an object, the code being called isn't determined until run time. The compiler *does* ensure that the function exists and performs type checking on the arguments and return value (languages of which this is not true are called *weakly typed*), but it doesn't know the exact code to execute.

To perform late binding, the compiler inserts a special bit of code in lieu of the absolute call. This code calculates the address of the code to execute using a pointer stored in the object itself. This pointer, called the *VPTR* in C++ and the *VMT pointer* in Turbo Pascal, points to a table of function addresses. These are the addresses of all the functions in this generic base type that have late-binding properties. Since each object contains its own pointer, it can behave differently according to the contents of that pointer. Thus, when you send a message to an object, the object actually does figure out what to do with the message.

Late binding requires extra code to calculate the function address and a short time in which to calculate it. Some programmers (especially C programmers, who are notorious for their fanatical views on efficiency) may object to this overhead. Some object-oriented languages force late binding for all functions, but in the spirit of C and Pascal you have a choice. You state that you want a function to have the flexibility of late-binding properties using the keyword *virtual* in C++ and Turbo Pascal; without the keyword, slightly more efficient early binding is performed.

You don't need to understand the meaning of *virtual* to use C++ or Turbo Pascal, but you can't do object-oriented programming without it. It's the key to the kingdom; once you understand how to use virtual functions, you'll understand OOP (which, although it may be a silly-sounding acronym, is useful partly because it keeps us humble). You'll find further illumination about *virtual* in the pages of this book.

Code Reuse

An issue that is often raised in object-oriented programming is code reuse. Many programmers find this confusing because they feel code reuse is already embodied in named subroutines (which we call *functions* in C++ and Pascal, although Pascal uses an additional subtype of *function* called a *procedure*). Since calling a function in more than one place reuses the code in that function, isn't that code reuse?

Although the answer to this may be "yes" in a discussion of pre-object-oriented languages, OOP takes it much further. Code reuse in object-oriented programming means type reuse. You reuse a type in two situations: when it satisfies your needs in the form it's in and when you can make it satisfy your needs with some small additions or modifications. The beauty of the second case is that you can make changes without touching the original code (a statement that at first sounds contradictory) using inheritance.

If you want to create a new type and you have one that does most of what you need, you can inherit the existing type into the new one, add new data and functions, and change the meaning of existing functions. This is a very powerful tool because it lets you make modifications and improvements without touching (or breaking) existing code. Any bugs that show up are automatically isolated to the new code. Code reuse in an object-oriented language is thus a fundamentally different and more useful concept than it is in procedural languages; it increases both your power and your flexibility.

Language Extensibility

Because we're effectively extending the language by creating new data types that the compiler treats like built-in types, the specter of the extensible language rears its head. Although some extensible languages like Forth are still popular in small circles, they are generally considered to be failures as general-purpose languages. That's because of the propensity of programmers to create their own languages, which is exactly what an extensible language is intended for. In a sense, it has many similarities to object-oriented programming because you modify an extensible language until it fits the problem you're trying to solve, and you add types to an OOP environment until they model the problem you're trying to solve.

The problem with extensible languages is that code written in a programmer's own version of that language tends to be write-only. Object-oriented languages don't suffer from this problem for two reasons.

First, extensible languages never made a clear distinction between the base language and the programmer's extensions to the language. Although some tried to determine the core of the language (and thus what you could expect to be there), agreement was difficult to reach, in part because there was never a good reason to draw the line on language extensions. In addition, you can change the basic meaning of almost anything in an extensible language like Forth, so you don't necessarily know if your environment has a function; if it does, you don't necessarily know what it does.

C++ and Turbo Pascal are hybrid OOP languages, which means they were created from existing languages. The existing languages have a distinct set of built-in types (although the programmers who use "pure" OOP languages like Smalltalk observe that the built-in types suffer from inadequacies absent in "real" OOP types; this can be rectified simply, though with some overhead, by creating new types from the built-in types). The compiler only knows about the built-in types until you tell it about the user-defined types you want to use. Thus, there's a clear line between the core of the language — what's built into the compiler — and an extension (always added at compile time). Neither the programmer nor the reader of the code will ever have any doubt where this line is. Pure languages like Smalltalk don't have this distinction, and the two primary flavors of Smalltalk differ in the types available in the basic system (which is notably vast; one of the obstacles to learning Smalltalk is its large library of types).

Second, the extensions in OOP languages are only in terms of types, not the fundamental control structures and operators, and the compiler checks to make sure instances of these types are used properly. Thus, you don't have the "shifting-sands" approach seen in extensible languages — the rules for type extension are very clear and are enforced by the compiler.

The bottom line is accountability — you always know how to find out what a piece of code means in an OOP language, whereas *anything* can be modified and changed in an extensible language without checking or any sort of audit trail. The reader of the code cannot be certain what the code means because it depends on the extended version of the language it's running on.

Advantages of Hybrid Languages

A hybrid OOP language has the disadvantage that its built-in types may behave slightly differently from user-defined types. In addition, some programmers complain about the dearth of user-defined types that come with a programming environment (in comparison to Smalltalk, which has many types). The latter will be rectified somewhat as standards develop, but languages like C++ and Turbo Pascal weren't meant to come with many libraries as much as to support many large and diverse libraries.

One might find fault with hybrid OOP languages, but certain features are undeniable advantages. First and foremost is the learning curve. Essentially, programmers in the non-object-oriented versions of the language can begin using the object-oriented versions immediately, albeit without using any of the new features.

Although it may be theoretically convenient to say "Throw away everything you know and learn it the right way," it's hardly practical. This is seen in the tremendous migration of C programmers to C++.

Not only is it comfortable for programmers who aren't ready for the full force of OOP, learning the new OOP features in the context of a familiar language seems much easier than learning an entirely new language and new concepts at the same time. The differences between the old and new ways of thinking are very clear, so programmers know when they're venturing into new territory. The final comfort is that they know they can always go back to the old style.

Not everything needs to be an object. Everything in a pure object-oriented language is an object, even the type definitions themselves. This is the object-oriented philosophy taken to the extreme. While it has a purist appeal, it isn't always practical. Sometimes you need a function or an ordinary chunk of memory; to be arbitrarily forced to make everything an object can be an unwieldy constraint.

Another advantage of hybrid OOP languages is that large bodies of existing code are still available. C++ is designed to compile ANSI C code with few or no changes, and Turbo Pascal is designed to compile previous Turbo Pascal with no changes at all (this is described later). Thus, you can move to OOP without losing previous work.

Philosophical Differences

This book attempts to highlight the similarities between C++ and Turbo Pascal, but I think it's also helpful to note the differences and evaluate their differing philosophies.

The ANSI C language has, by necessity, been a compromise between the many divergent implementations of the C language that propagated as a result of the original, incompletely specified language. Although the ANSI C committee recognized the problems and holes in the resulting language, they didn't feel they could fill those holes without breaking significant amounts of existing code.

C++ has always had a single definition, created by its inventor, Bjarne Stroustrup. The definition is verified and formalized by the actions of the ANSI C++ committee, but there has never been the divergence experienced by C; the definition and original implementation came from Stroustrup and company at AT&T and has gone almost directly to the ANSI C++ committee. Although C++ is designed to compile as much existing C code as possible without change, it is also designed to produce very large systems, and this requires more strict support for safety. Thus, holes in the C language were filled so the compiler could catch errors that would otherwise go unnoticed. Closing up these holes has restricted the C code that can be compiled. This is a safer subset of existing C code, and C programmers will notice small differences in the language. I feel most people will see these differences as improvements, but they will definitely notice that C++ is not C.

In addition, some basic philosophies have been adhered to in the design of C++ that give a different feel to the language — in particular, the idea that you should never have uninitialized variables in a program. You can define variables at any point in a scope and wait until you have all the necessary information before defining the variable. Also, the compiler automatically generates calls to constructors (special functions that initialize a variable). The constructors ensure that both the data members and the VPTR are initialized. Philosophies like this have a definite impact on the way you program.

In Turbo Pascal, the design philosophy was very different. The intent was to leave the core language absolutely unchanged and make sure users who didn't want to know about OOP were unaffected by the additions to the language. No programs need to be modified because of the changes. This approach is very insightful but has distinctly different goals. Since type checking in Pascal was already quite strong, no major holes remain to be closed up in that area. However, Pascal would need to be written and compiled much differently to ensure initialized variables. The *VAR* section makes it very difficult to define and initialize variables at any point in a block and to call constructors at the point of definition; the programmer must call them explicitly at some later point. If they're forgotten, the initialization won't take place. This is particularly bad if the variable contains a VMT pointer.

The Turbo Pascal programmer must be vigilant. It's unfortunate, but I don't see how it could have been circumvented without changing the language so significantly that it would have violated the goal of full code compatibility.

In this book, the differences are only pointed out when it's absolutely necessary (as in the need to call constructors in Pascal). The differences don't influence the effectiveness of the basic OOP ideas in either language.

Design

The analogy of the Tao with object-oriented programming is most obvious when you're making a first cut at a problem or thinking about OOP design. Programmers have become so accustomed to thinking in terms of complexity — of the hardware, in the design process, in the implementation, and when modeling and documenting a system — that their first reaction to OOP is often something like "Where are the bits and bytes and *for* loops?" There's great resistance when you're presented with code that describes the system you're trying to solve rather than the system in which you're trying to solve it.

In addition, we have somehow been taught that starting to program before solving the problem on paper is heresy. This attitude is understandable; we've all seen the spaghetti code created by programmers who dove in without any plan at all. Coding by the seat of your pants works with small problems but stops working when you cross some mysterious size boundary. However, the concept of planning is usually taken to the opposite, impractical extreme. Everyone talks about it, but in the end it appears to require too much time, so people go back to programming by the seat of their pants.

Too much planning is impractical, anyway — we learn through experimentation, not by doing thought examples as the Greeks were wont to do with their physics. One of the benefits of OOP is that user-defined data types tend to partition a program into stable pieces; procedural programming requires programmer discipline to prevent an unstable design, while OOP supports a tendency toward increasing stability. Parts of the program that are unstable won't affect parts that are, since user-defined data types focus behaviors of the program in tightly coupled areas of code.

The two fundamental design guidelines of programming, high coupling and low cohesion, are still valid but must be applied (like everything else in OOP) to entire types rather than individual functions.

In the philosophy of the Tao, the focus is on the path rather than the destination, the process rather than the goal. The same, I think, is true of OOP design and problem-solving. If you focus on a particular implementation, you may tie yourself to a solution that you later find to be unworkable; you may not want to end up where you originally thought you did. That is, focusing more on the goal than on the path may mean you'll end up in the wrong place because you ignored valuable information — you already had all those design documents and your mind was made up. The way of the Tao is to let the path show you the way. Applying this philosophy to object-oriented programming means letting the process of solving the problem show you what the objects should be and what they should look like.

The bulk of the last chapter (on design) is derived from notes I made while musing about the design problem in OOP versus structured techniques. (Like all zealots, I couldn't understand why all programmers didn't take up this so obviously correct way of developing programs; only later did I figure out that programmers like to program, not write seven different types of documentation.) I keep coming to the conclusion that the best model for the program is the program itself. Every time I try to come up with a different representation, I seem to end up with something more complicated than just writing down the type declarations.

That's why I emphasize that the best approach for object-oriented programmers is to start writing down type declarations and fill out from there. Don't worry if you don't know everything when you start creating the types; as you develop the system, you'll see the answers and the details will sort themselves out. This is very different from the idea that you must know everything before you write a single line of code, but it's one of the reasons OOP is so powerful — it's more reflective and supportive of the way programmers actually do things (they write code).

Buying In

Programmers often feel someone is trying to sell them something. There *are* the traditional folks who are simply trying to make money, but the more persistent and zealous ones are those who try to get "mind share." Choosing a language involves both, so the efforts heat up even more.

More intellectually sophisticated programming languages than C++ and Turbo Pascal certainly exist, and some languages are easier to learn; both types have been pushed as "better." As effective as the sell jobs have been, we aren't selling soap here — programmers are a sophisticated audience, and a suspicious one. It doesn't take long for negative reviews to get back to the pack, and a language that once seemed promising becomes mediocre or, worse, laughable. You can't hide for long the fact that a language has been created by someone with a particular bent or background, an axe to grind, or a single good idea. Programmers will tolerate some flaws and limitations in a new language, but not too many, and not if they're capricious, gratuitous, or myopic.

Programmers often switch to object-oriented languages when offered C++ and Turbo Pascal, even if they resisted earlier languages, because that feeling of "rightness" has been struck: It's not too different, the learning time of the programmer has not been considered unimportant in favor of the proper language purity, and those programmers who value such issues as efficiency, ROMability, real-time, and robustness have not been dismissed. As much as possible, the practical issues as well as the desire for conceptual purity have been mixed together in these languages, and programmers haven't taken long to see that it's (finally) the right compromise — that is, until the next great concept in computer science shows up (multineural nonlinear persistent room-temperature-superconducting C++, anyone?).

Programmers work out a model in their heads of how things work and have some trouble dislodging that model once they've tested it and come to believe in it. This prevents them from making big mistakes, like switching to a language that's too limited for their needs, but it also significantly slows down the shift to a more powerful way of thinking. When I asked Andrew Koenig to name the most frequently encountered problem among people learning OOP, he said it was the belief that a programming language is for manipulating pieces of memory rather than manipulating concepts.

A language provides an interface between us and some machine-implemented agents. A good language attempts to insulate us, as much as possible, from the details and limitations of the particular agents (without preventing us from getting our work done). As long as we persist in doing assembly-language programming in whatever high-level language we're using, we'll be constrained to solving a small subset of problems. The really big problems are solved by dealing with the concepts, not some intermediate representation of the concepts (chunks of memory, data-flow diagrams, structure charts, and so on).

OOP languages support this way of thinking about problems, and languages like Smalltalk may even force you to think about problems this way (but require the effort of learning an entirely foreign language and set of rules). In C++ and Turbo Pascal, you aren't forced. As simple and optional as the language extensions may seem, remember that they are only *support* for OOP and won't make your programs better unless you can eventually shift your thinking from bytes to concepts. This book should help you make that shift.

Bruce Eckel
December 1990

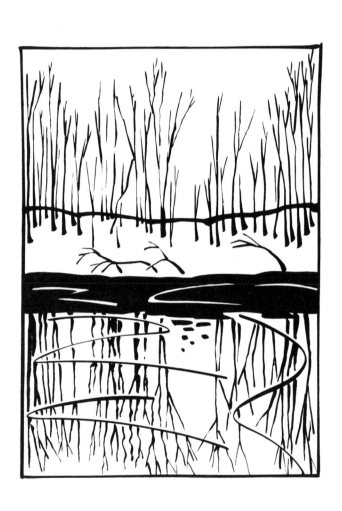

CHAPTER 1

Great Journeys, Single Steps

The soft overcomes the hard; the gentle overcomes the rigid.
Everyone knows this is true, but few can put it into practice.
— Lao-tzu

What makes you you, and what are your boundaries?
— Douglas R. Hofstadter
and Daniel C. Dennett

Ancient Chinese philosophers believed in a unifying reality called the *Tao* (pronounced "dow"). These philosophers of the Tao, or Way, emphasized that the world is not a static entity, but a dynamic process. The objects that compose the world are reflections of that process—in flux and ever-changing. Thus, the ability to model or capture an object's essence is illusory; we really only capture a bit of it for a short while.

A computer program is a process, a tool, a way to model, capture, or simulate part of the world. In traditional programming, static concepts impose themselves on a dynamic world. It becomes difficult to model the world or modify the model. Object-oriented programming is a major step toward making programming and the programs themselves dynamic. Using object-oriented programming techniques, you can design programs that are better suited for modeling a dynamic world, create and destroy complex processes at both compile time and run time, and design programs as if they evolved (which they do).

Object-oriented programming adds three key features to structured programming. These features let you more clearly envision a program as a dynamic process and plan for its inevitable evolution. While most programming systems force you to accept a static model of the world as the best you can do, object-oriented programming assumes that the world and the programs you use to model it will change and evolve. It is both a new way to write programs and a new way to think about the interaction of programs and the world . . . both a method and a philosophy.

Object-oriented programming techniques allow you to analyze problems using a programming model that more closely mirrors the way you believe the world works. If you can map programs more closely to the world, you can revise them more easily as the world evolves. You can design programs with a built-in capacity for evolution. Object-oriented programming also allows you to create general reusable objects. Programmers can be more productive and project managers a bit more sane.

But there's more to it than that. Object-oriented programming isn't just one way of programming or solving problems; it's a continuum of ideas about programming and design. It adds to rather than replaces structured programming. In some ways, it's even more structured than structured programming. It assimilates the best previous attempts at modularity and data abstraction into the most powerful programming model yet.

About the Book

This book consists of:

- Seven chapters (each containing short examples in C++ and Turbo Pascal)
- A glossary
- An appendix of interesting developments in object-oriented programming and other matters that don't fit into the main text
- A reference list of books and software to help you pursue object-oriented programming
- An index.

Chapters 1 and 2 introduce the general features composing an object-oriented language. Chapters 3, 4, 5, and 6 refine the concepts introduced in those chapters. Chapter 7 completes the picture, summing up the implications of object-oriented programming and describing a method for incorporating object-oriented programming techniques in applications programming.

Examples will be given in both C++ and Turbo Pascal. Chaos and complexity theory, phase and state spaces, agents (secret and otherwise), spreadsheets, expert systems, neural networks, and intelligent system design are a few of the ideas we'll explore. I think you're going to use object-oriented programming to develop your own ideas. I do.

Although C++ and Turbo Pascal (with object extensions) are conceptually very similar, their designers and other writers describe them differently. Throughout this book, I'll try to use language that's consistent with the AT&T C++ 2.1 specification (the primary base document for the ANSI C++ committee), the ANSI C specification, and the Turbo C++ and Turbo Pascal manuals.

Choose Your Language

C++ and Turbo Pascal use different terms to represent similar concepts:

Concept	C++	Turbo Pascal
data structure	struct	record
user-defined type	class	object type
variable of user-defined type	object	instance
data field	member	field
behavior	member function, method	method

Some languages, such as Smalltalk, Actor, and Eiffel, effectively treat everything as objects. We sometimes call these languages *pure*. Others, such as C++ and Turbo Pascal — the hybrids — extend structured languages to handle objects. You have the option of using object types in a hybrid language, but you can still use functions and ordinary data structures.

Although C++ and Turbo Pascal are two of the most popular object-oriented languages, true to the spirit of the Tao, there are many other paths to choose from. Each path takes a slightly different approach to the same goal: a better way to create software. The "pure" or completely object-oriented languages treat everything according to the same principles. This makes the languages consistent but sometimes a bit awkward, especially for those of us who have been using traditional languages such as C and Pascal.

For example, in Smalltalk, even simple code such as adding numbers is considered object-oriented: Simply send a plus message to a number object to add to itself. Or consider the case of a traditional *if* statement. In Smalltalk, this is written as an *IfTrue* message to a *Condition* object that evaluates to true or false.

Languages such as Actor and Eiffel are more understandable to traditional programmers. These languages use enough "syntactic sugar," or embellishments, to make them accessible to those who are familiar with C or Pascal. At the same time, they retain the elegance and consistency of a completely object-oriented world.

You can use any of these languages to explore the world of object-oriented programming. If you're already a C or Pascal programmer, C++ and Turbo Pascal are great ways to get your foot in the OOP door.

I'm assuming you already know how to program in C, C++, or Turbo Pascal, so we won't spend time going over basic programming concepts. Instead, we'll focus on the object-oriented aspects of C++ and Turbo Pascal.

Object-oriented programming will undoubtedly bend your mind a little, but if you already know C or Pascal, the bending will be more fun than difficult.

Objects and Actions

The world consists of objects and actions. Objects (or *nouns*, in grammatical terms) possess attributes or characteristics. Actions (or *verbs*) express or exhibit behavior.

> The wind blows.
> A bird sings.
> A window opens.

In programming terms, data is the characteristics of an object and operations (functions or procedures) are its behaviors. An object-oriented programming language encapsulates an object's characteristics and behaviors within a single block of source code. Putting operations and behaviors in one place makes good sense; it's safer and more convenient. Combining data with the operations to manipulate that data into a single package is called *encapsulation*.

Object-oriented programming languages give programmers the power to create their own object types, which the compiler treats just like built-in types. You build complex types from simpler ones that share characteristics and behaviors. Programmers have been creating new types all along — by collecting variables into *struct*s (in C) and *record*s (in Pascal). The only difference is that the functions to manipulate these types have been ordinary ones.

The new object type looks a lot like its data-only counterpart (*struct* or *record*). But it's self-contained: Data and the operations to manipulate the data are encapsulated in one package. In C++ we call this new type a *class* — a *struct* plus functions to manipulate the data fields. In Turbo Pascal, we call it an *object type* — a record and the functions and procedures to manipulate the data fields. For simplicity, I'll refer to functions and procedures in Pascal as *functions*, since a procedure is just a specific type of function. In object-oriented languages, the functions are brought into the object type, so it's not surprising that this new type — the C++ *class* or the Turbo Pascal object type — looks very similar to C *struct*s and Pascal *record*s.

In C++, you might declare a *struct* like this:

```
struct aStruct {
  char Name[10];
  int X,Y;
};
```

In Turbo Pascal, you could declare a *record* like this:

```
type
record1 = aRecord;
aRecord = record
  Name : string;
  X,Y : integer;
end;
```

In C++, you can declare a *class* like this:

```
class aClass {
public:
  int X,Y;
  void doSomethingWithXandY();
};
```

Public is a C++ keyword meaning "anyone can use it." Things that aren't public can only be accessed by class methods.

You define a variable of type *aClass* like this:

```
aClass cv;
```

and a pointer (a variable that holds the address of another variable) like this:

```
aClass * cp = &cv;
```

In Turbo Pascal, you define an object like this:

```
type
anObject = object
  X,Y : integer;
  procedure doSomethingWithXandY;
end;
```

A variable of type *anObject* looks like this:

```
var ov: anObject;
```

We can declare a pointer, *op*, and get the address of *ov* like this:

```
var op: ^anObject;
op = @ov;
```

X and *Y* are data fields, and *doSomethingWithXandY* is a method for manipulating *anObject*. Notice that everything in Turbo Pascal is the equivalent of *public* in C++.

To access members of a user-defined type variable, you use exactly the same selection operators available for *struct*s in C and *record*s in Pascal — "." for variables and "->" for pointers to variables in C++:

```
cv.X = 2;
cv.doSomethingWithXandY();          /* function call! */
cp->x = 2;
cp->doSomethingWithXandY();
```

and "." or a *with* statement and "^." for pointers to variables in Turbo Pascal:

```
ov.X := 2;
op^.doSomethingWithXandY;           {* function call! *}

With ov do
  begin
    X:= 2;
    Y:= 4;
    doSomethingWithXandY;
  end;
```

An object type consists of everything you know about it. Data and functions are together in one box. If a *struct* or *record* is a container for characteristics, then this new type (class or object) is a container for characteristics and behaviors.

Notice that you don't have to pass *X* and *Y* to *doSomethingWithXandY*; it already knows about them because they're contained within the same type (they share a local scope). Everything in a user-defined object type (characteristics and behaviors) is shared. It's like a small town — everyone knows about everyone else within the city limits.

This combining of data and code in one object is an important extension of C++ translation units (source-code files) and Turbo Pascal units. (We'll refer to both simply as *units*.) Programs consist of collections of units, which contain definitions of classes, objects, functions, and variables. At the simplest level, these new object types suggest a new way to organize code. Combining data and code — encapsulation — is one of the cornerstones of object-oriented programming.

You classify objects in the world into types and extend your knowledge by assigning the characteristics and behaviors you know (from previous types) to new object types. Using object-oriented programming techniques, you build programs in a similar manner: by creating base types and deriving more complex types from them.

A World of Objects

Offer a child a new type of clothing, and she'll determine that it can be worn and probably try to put it on. Given a new type of container, you know there must be a way to open and close it (even if it's child- and/or programmer-proof).

Because you've driven bicycles, cars, boats, or airplanes, you know that vehicles share many characteristics while differing in others. For example, any vehicle can be steered. Although the steering mechanisms differ among vehicles, you can generalize about them. Then, faced with a new type of vehicle (for example, a spaceship), you can surmise that there's probably some way to steer it. We can say that *vehicle* is a base type and *spaceship* is a derived type.

Object-oriented programming languages mirror these facts about the real world by letting you create abstract data types. You can create a base type to represent behaviors and characteristics common to derived types. With inheritance, you can create a hierarchy of types derived from this base type.

An object is a special kind of variable of a new type that you or some other programmer has created. User-defined object types behave just like built-in types — they have internal data and external operations. For example, a floating-point number has an exponent, mantissa, and sign bit and knows how to add itself to another floating-point number.

User-defined object types contain user-defined data (characteristics) and operations (behaviors). Although they look almost exactly like functions, user-defined operations are called *methods*. To call one of these methods, you make a general request of the object; this is known as "sending a message to the object." For example, to stop a car object, you send it a *stop* message. Note that this is based on our notion of encapsulation; we tell the object what to do, but the details of how it works have been encapsulated.

About Inheritance

Encapsulation is helpful, but there's more to object-oriented programming than that. How do you extend the functionality of an object? Go in and change the code and introduce new bugs? Not if you can help it. Once you've defined a new base type, you can build on it using inheritance. When a new type (called a *derived type*) inherits from a base type, the derived type automatically gets all the characteristics and behaviors of the base type.

Object types can share characteristics and behaviors. These shared factors can be collected into a common type known as a *base type*. Apples, oranges, and bananas are all types of edible fruit. They have different specific characteristics, but each has a color and each can be eaten. The base type, *edible fruit*, encapsulates the common characteristics *has color* and *is edible*.

The act of eating may be different in each case. You have to peel a banana before eating it, and you eat everything but the peel. You don't have to peel an apple, and you can eat the peel, but you don't eat the core.

You might be tempted to assume that you always use inheritance to add data attributes and behavior to objects. In many cases, however, composition is preferable. The data and behavior of an object are best thought of as those things that are directly inherited, plus the capabilities of the fields (also called *members* or *instance variables*). For example, a *car* object type inherits from the more abstract *vehicle* object type, but a car does not inherit from *engine*, *wheels*, and *transmission*. Rather, a car is composed of those additional objects. Thus, objects can contain other objects, just like in the real world.

When deciding how to create objects, you must always balance what is appropriately inherited with what is better encapsulated through the use of methods and fields. Newcomers often make the mistake of overusing inheritance when composition would be more appropriate. The key question to ask yourself when using inheritance is: "Is my derived object type inherently similar to the base type?" Only use inheritance when the answer is yes, and consider using composition in other cases. Derivation and composition allow you to reuse old code without introducing new bugs. This means you can program much faster and more efficiently.

Object-oriented programming is a way to build family trees (or hierarchies) for data structures. Any type can have a long family tree, but in C++ a class can have more than one immediate ancestor; we call this *multiple inheritance* (see Figure 1-1). In Turbo Pascal, an object can have only one immediate ancestor; we call this *single inheritance*.

If inheritance sounds good, you might assume that multiple inheritance is even better. In fact, multiple inheritance is one of those hotly debated philosophical issues among language designers. Most OOP languages — including Pascal with Objects, Objective-C, Smalltalk, and Actor — implement only single inheritance. Eiffel and C++, on the other hand, support multiple inheritance. Generally speaking, nothing can be done in a multiple-inheritance language that can't also be done in a single-inheritance language, though it's sometimes a bit more work.

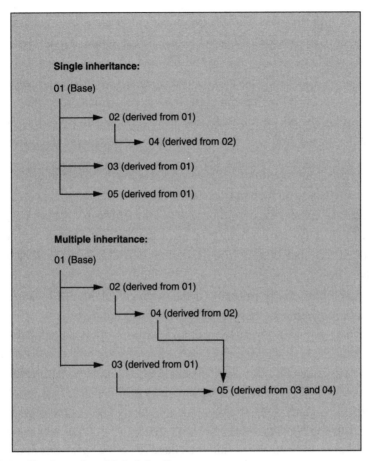

Figure 1-1. Single and multiple inheritance.

A difficulty arises with multiple inheritance when you combine several object types, each of which defines the same methods or fields. Suppose two object types, *Sound* and *Graphic*, are combined into a new object type called *Multimedia. Sound* has the data fields *pitch, duration,* and *voice* and the methods *play, rescale, load,* and *store. Graphic* has the data fields *bitmap, size,* and *color* and the methods *draw, rescale, load,* and *store.* When you combine these into the new object type, *Multimedia,* there's a conflict between the methods *rescale, load,* and *store.*

What does it mean for a *Multimedia* object to rescale itself? That depends on what you want to happen. Does it mean to rescale the sound at a different pitch (as with *Sound*) or fit in a smaller space (as with *Graphic*)? What if you attempt to load or store a *Multimedia* object? Should it store itself as a *Sound* or a *Graphic* or write out both components? If it writes out both components, which order should be used? Should this order always be followed when there are conflicts? In most multiple-inheritance languages, you end up writing extra code to resolve the difficulty.

The problem is one of ambiguity. It may not be clear to the compiler in a multiple-inheritance language which operation should take precedence when conflicts arise. More importantly, even if the compiler resolves the ambiguity, you as the programmer may have difficulty remembering the rules, particularly when debugging. Some language designers feel that multiple inheritance is essential. Most view it as a double-edged sword: It gives power and flexibility, but at the same time it can increase the complexity of programs. It has been called "the Goto of the 1990s" because it adds convenience but can easily be misused.

When you want to implement in a single-inheritance language a new object type that looks like it needs multiple inheritance, use composition. This usually means inheriting from the most appropriate object type and using a field to contain the object of the other type. If we combined *Sound* and *Graphic*, we would probably choose to define the *Multimedia* type to have two fields, each of which contained a *Sound* and *Graphic* object. We would then need to define "pass-through" methods that specified unambiguously what would happen when a *Multimedia* object got a message such as *rescale*, *load*, or *store*.

Neither multiple inheritance nor single inheritance is perfect in all cases, and both can require a little bit of extra code to make up for differences in how they work. There will always be times when the tool you use takes you down the wrong path, but it's important to recognize the beauty of the path you take and use the tool as it's meant to be used. Perhaps a future path will go beyond the notion of multiple inheritance and take us to even better places.

Building a New Type

Let's say you've created a base type in C++:

```
class base {
public:
  int X,Y;
  void doSomethingWithXandY();
};
```

or in Turbo Pascal:

```
base = object
  X,Y: integer;
  procedure doSomethingWithXandY;
end;
```

Now you want to build a new type derived from the existing base type. You want the derived type to be identical to the base type, with one exception: You'll extend *base* by adding a method called *doSomethingElse*.

You build *derived* simply and quickly by inheriting from *base*. In C++:

```
class derived : public base {
public:
  void doSomethingElse();
};
```

In Turbo Pascal:

```
derived = object (base)
  procedure doSomethingElse;
end;
```

Since *derived* inherits all the data and methods of *base*, you don't need to redefine them; you simply tell the compiler you want to derive a new type (*derived*) from a base type (*base*) and add the new method. Now you can *doSomethingWithXandY* and *doSomethingElse* to variables of type *derived*. In C++:

```
main() {
  derived d;
  d.x = 5;
  d.y = 8;
  d.doSomethingWithXandY();
  d.doSomethingElse();
}
```

In Turbo Pascal:

```
var
d: derived;

With d do
  begin
    X:= 5;
    Y:= 8;
    doSomethingWithXandY;
    doSomethingElse;
  end;
```

Notice again that you don't have to pass *X* and *Y* to *doSomethingElse*; it inherited knowledge of them, along with everything else, from *base*.

Inheritance lets you build very complex data types without repeating a lot of code. The new type simply inherits a base level of characteristics and behavior from an ancestor. It can also reimplement, or overwrite, any method it chooses. This reimplementation of base-type methods in derived types is fundamental to the concept of polymorphism, which we'll get to in a moment.

Inheritance is useful for two reasons. The first is simple: If you're given a working object type that doesn't do exactly what you want, you can create a new object type from it with inheritance and add a few characteristics. Not only can you program quickly, you can isolate the existing code (which works) from your new, experimental code (which may not).

Inheritance Among OOP Languages

Interestingly enough, object-oriented languages themselves exhibit inheritance as they build on concepts introduced in previous languages. Most traditional structured languages, including C, Pascal, and PL/I, have been heavily influenced by Algol. Simula, the first OOP language, also inherited characteristics of Algol but added the concepts of objects, classes, and messages. All OOP languages inherit some of the characteristics and behavior of programming in Simula, either directly or from its descendant, Smalltalk.

Although some of the inheritance is clearly from a single ancestor (for example, BCPL begat B, which begat C), many of the languages borrowed from two or more ancestors, demonstrating multiple inheritance. This is especially true of the hybrid languages, including Turbo Pascal with Objects and C++, which combine characteristics and behavior of object-oriented languages with those of their traditional base languages, Pascal and C. That doesn't mean Turbo Pascal with Objects has multiple inheritance, just that it's built on the concepts of the languages that preceded it.

Overriding Behavior and Data

Inheritance lets us automatically use the data and methods of a base type. Even though you inherit methods, you can always override them to achieve some different behavior. For example, you might create a descendant of a bar-chart type that draws in three dimensions. You're not locked into the implementation found in the base type, but what if you want to use the inherited method and do some new actions? You could simply define the new method to call the ancestor's routine. You have the choice of calling the ancestor routine either before or after the new actions.

What if you want to "subtract" behavior that you inherit? You can do that by defining a dummy method that does nothing at all. However, if you find yourself writing lots of dummy methods to subtract behavior, it may be a sign that the base type should be broken down further so you can inherit only the pieces you need.

Overriding the methods in an object is easy. Overriding the fields is a little more difficult and requires more careful planning. For example, you can't normally override the built-in types in *struct*s or *record*s without using variant record types. The key is to make fields that must be overridden into objects themselves. For example, if you have a car hierarchy and different car models use different types of transmissions, then *Transmission* itself should be an object type with derived types for *Automatic*, *Manual*, *FiveSpeed*, and so on. It may not always be obvious when to divide things into objects, but when you start creating objects that contain other objects, you're on the road to object-oriented programming.

The second use of inheritance concerns the behavior of derived object types that descend from the same base. When you learn to steer a bicycle, you learn something that can also be applied to a car or boat. When you pilot any of these vehicles, you don't have to think about which type of vehicle it is to steer it — you turn the controls in one direction, and the vehicle moves in that direction. Since this is true in the world, why shouldn't it be true of programming as well?

About Polymorphism

Let's represent this system with a base object type called *vehicle* and derived object types called *bicycle*, *car*, and *boat*. Any vehicle can be steered, and vehicles do different things to steer themselves depending on their type. *Vehicle* can respond to a message called *steer*, so any type that inherits *vehicle* can also accept that message.

Thus, bicycles, cars, and boats can be steered because they're vehicles, although the method each specific type uses when it gets the *steer* message is different. This is called *polymorphism*. You tell the vehicle to steer itself (send it a *steer* message), and it figures out what to do with the message.

Why is this so important? Because you don't have to reimplement everything each time you create a new type of vehicle; you build on the existing objects. An object-oriented program that steers vehicles doesn't have to be rewritten just because it needs to handle a new type of vehicle. It already knows that any vehicle can respond to the *steer* message and act accordingly.

Using polymorphism to create extensible programs is important because programmers can't know everything about a program or the problem it needs to solve while developing the program. Programs need to change in response to new information.

Word processors didn't know about desktop publishing when they were created; new features had to be added as user needs changed. The need to change and evolve has been a nemesis of software development because change is expensive and the inability to change often leads to obsolescence.

Change must be considered an integral part of a program. New information might come from understanding a system in a new way or because the problem changes in the real world. Either way, change is inevitable. Polymorphism reflects that by letting you create extensible programs.

Behaviors like steering a vehicle and opening a container can be common to a group of types but implemented differently for each (such as the mechanisms for steering a bicycle and steering a car). Using polymorphism, you can create a system that knows vehicles can be steered but not how a particular vehicle will be steered; those details can come later. The system is extensible because we can add new types of vehicles (and new ways of steering) without redesigning the program.

The ability to create abstract data types is a powerful one. Because people view the world in terms of types, representing a real-world system as a program of base and derived types is a natural process. Ideally, the model of the system in the computer is a direct mapping of the system in the real world. This means that if the system in the real world changes, it's easy to change the model in the computer. This simplicity makes software design, development, and maintenance faster and cheaper.

Abstract data types also tend to localize changes in a system. Using traditional function-oriented techniques, you may make a change that propagates bugs throughout the system. But changes in an object-oriented system tend to be localized in an abstract data type. Since the data and functions are in one package, changes aren't as likely to propagate bugs outside that package. Therefore, you can change part of a working system without disrupting the rest.

When we talk about objects, we often talk about the protocol they understand. We can think of protocol as the set of messages an object can respond to. Generally, you'll find that objects that share a common base type or are compatible with each other have the same protocol. When designing your objects, try to follow a consistent, generic protocol so that your objects are more easily reused.

Inheritance and polymorphism let you create a base type that establishes a common interface to a group of types (which are created by inheritance from the base type). This interface defines which messages an object can receive and what the protocol is.

If your system understands and uses the interface to the base without knowing the particulars of the derived types, it can easily be extended. If you need to add a type to an existing system, you simply derive it from the base type. The system only uses the base interface, so it immediately knows what to do with your new type.

You can easily create any number of variables of a type, even at run time. Libraries of abstract data types are easy to reuse in new applications and can be extended when used in conjunction with inheritance, even if you don't have the source code for the library.

For example, if you're creating a motel management system using someone else's general-purpose room type, you can create your own type, *motel_room*, by inheriting from *room* and adding characteristics and behavior to tell the user whether the room is occupied, has been cleaned, needs painting, and so on. Thus, you can easily reuse code by using an existing type or by inheriting and adding to an existing type.

When you call a method for an object, you send a message to the object. You think of a message as a function call. Why the distinction between sending a message and calling a function? Normally, it's just like a function call: You knew when you wrote the code what would be executed for that call.

With polymorphism, however, the code to be executed isn't determined until run time. You can send a message to an object of a generic type and let the object figure out which method to call. "Put on the item of clothing" will evoke different responses depending on whether the item is a hat or a shoe.

Polymorphism means that a method can have one name that's shared throughout an object-type hierarchy. Each object type may have a different implementation for the method. The name of the method is the same for each object type, but what it does is different.

Suppose you want to define deri*ved2*, which inherits the data and methods from *derived* and reimplements the method *doSomethingElse*. You define it as follows in C++:

```
class derived2 : public derived {
public:
  void doSomethingElse();
};
```

and in Turbo Pascal:

```
derived2 = object (derived)
  procedure doSomethingElse;
end;
```

Now when you use a variable of type *derived2*, it will inherit the data fields from *derived* but can use its own *doSomethingElse* method.

When you send a message to an object, the compiler first looks to see if the object's type definition contains the method you want. If it finds the method in the type definition, that's what it uses. If the type definition doesn't contain the method, the compiler searches the inheritance hierarchy until it finds the appropriate method. If it doesn't find the method in any ancestor, it reports an error.

Making the compiler search through the inheritance hierarchy for the correct method takes time and can decrease performance. The overhead is generally not that great, especially in hybrid languages like C++ and Turbo Pascal. However, there will be times when you want to reduce the impact by optimizing your code.

Although we think of inheritance as requiring a search up the hierarchy to find the correct method, this technique would have disastrous results for large applications; the more you used inheritance, the slower your program would get. No object-oriented language that I know of uses this kind of linear search. Instead, an efficient indirect function call is used so that only one additional instruction is required on a method call. In most cases, less code is required to do this "call indirect" than to mimic the flexibility of object-oriented programming using an *if*, *switch*, or *case* statement.

Static and Dynamic Binding

Each object created so far uses statically bound methods. Static binding (also called *early binding*) means the compiler resolves all references to functions by the time the program is loaded. When you call a statically bound method, the compiler figures out exactly which function to call at compile time.

With polymorphism, you want to send a message to an object and let the object figure out which method to use. What you're asking the compiler to do is resolve some references at run time. This is called *late* or *dynamic binding*.

Why is late binding important? Because it lets you defer decisions and connections until run time, thus making the system more flexible and easier to extend. It also means we can give our objects general requests, and they can determine how to respond. We tell the objects *what* to do, and they figure out *how* to do it.

To resolve references to methods at run time, you create virtual methods. To create a virtual method in C++, add the keyword *virtual* to a function in the base class:

```
class aClass {
public:
   int X,Y;
   virtual void doSomethingWithXandY();
};
```

That's it; dynamic binding happens automatically for *doSomethingWithXandY* in all classes derived from *aClass*. But there's a catch: A method can't be statically bound in one type and virtual in another. You must anticipate that by declaring these methods as virtual from the beginning.

In Turbo Pascal, the story is slightly different — you add the keyword *virtual* to the method and include a special procedure, called a *constructor*, within the object (constructors happen automatically in C++). A constructor sets up the machinery for virtual methods and specifies how a new object type will be initialized.

Methods must also be declared as virtual in all inherited types. For example, you must declare *doSomethingWithXandY* as virtual at its earliest declaration and in all subsequent declarations:

```
derived = object(base)
   constructor init;
   procedure doSomethingWithXandY; virtual;
end;

anObject4 = object(derived2)
   constructor init;
   procedure doSomethingElse; virtual;
end;
```

Virtual methods allow derived types to have their own versions of a base-type method. This is a powerful (but sometimes thorny) aspect of object-oriented programming, one we'll return to again and again as we learn more about the Tao of objects.

Dynamic Programming

Object-oriented languages support a dynamic style of programming, allowing variables to be created and destroyed as easily at run time as at compile time. Think about it: The situations where you know all the types and quantities of objects while you're writing the program are really the special cases. In general, you don't know those factors. In a CAD system, for example, you don't know until the program is running which shapes or types of shapes the user will want to display. Object-oriented programming is dynamic; it lets you design systems that are flexible enough to accommodate change.

C and Pascal programmers have been able to program dynamically for a long time. Dynamic memory allocation and pointers allow you to get and release space for variables at run time. You can decide when to create and destroy the variables and how many variables to use. You use a pointer to hold the address of a dynamically allocated chunk of memory (you can think of a pointer as simply a way to change, at run time, the storage used by an identifier).

Unfortunately, dynamically allocated memory in C and Pascal is a poor relation to a real variable. You have to treat dynamic memory as a special case, making it harder and less reliable to use. In C++ and Turbo Pascal, the ability to create and destroy real variables at run time was considered so important that it's now in the core of those languages in the form of constructors and destructors. When you create a new, user-defined object type, making a dynamic variable of that type is as easy as making an automatic variable.

This means you can easily build an object-oriented program that doesn't need to know the number or type of objects involved in a problem before it begins to solve it. This idea fits beautifully with the world, where you seldom know all the tools you'll need when you begin working on a project. Object-oriented languages allow you to write programs that adapt to new situations.

Another View

You might find it helpful to think of an object as a little program. It has its own internal data and an interface through which you request operations and information. This is how you use, for example, a word processor (an object), which manages its own data. With the keyboard, you send the word processor such messages as "insert this character" and "delete that word."

Writing an object-oriented program is also like using a computer that allows you to run more than one program at once. You might use a communication program to fetch data, a spreadsheet to analyze it, and a word processor to prepare a report. Although you can (in theory, at least) write any of these programs yourself, you don't have to. It's easier to use programs someone else has written.

When you request data (a report, for example), you only want to see the report. Building a program using objects is similar. You "run" objects (just as you run programs) that perform various tasks. You may write the code for these objects or use someone else's. The program consists of objects and the messages you send them.

By now, you should be getting the message that a program is a static implementation of a solution. Object-oriented programming is a process for anticipating change in programs, one that lets them adapt to new situations.

Object Types

Although structured languages such as Pascal, C, and Modula-2 allow you to combine data and functions in distinct packages called *units*, *files*, or *modules*, they don't let you manipulate these packages of code as if they were built-in types.

Built-in types are special because the compiler knows how to handle them before you ever write a line of code. In contrast, the compiler must learn how to handle types that aren't built in.

THE TAO OF OBJECTS

Units, files, and modules do help organize and coordinate code, but they don't explicitly establish or maintain relationships among their components. Neither the data nor the functions in a module, unit, or file are explicitly protected. Thus, unless you declare data locally (within functions), any function in any module can manipulate and possibly corrupt it. If you declare a data element locally, you make it safer but limit access to a single function. If you declare it globally, everyone can get at it — definitely a dilemma.

Object-oriented languages give you a way out by introducing a new kind of structure that protects data elements and creates specific relationships for them. We call this new structure a *user-defined object type*, or just plain *object type*. The compiler knows about object types and treats them as if they were built into the language. Although object types are the key to object-oriented programming, not all object-oriented languages treat them exactly the same way.

For example, C++ and Turbo Pascal differ significantly in how they let you access the data in a user-defined type. C++ gives you more control over the degree to which the data and methods of a type can be accessed. The keywords *private*, *public*, *protected*, and *friend* are used to control access.

- *Public* means that anyone can use it. Any methods following the keyword can only be accessed by methods declared within the same class.

- *Private* means that any members following the keyword can be accessed only by member functions declared within the same class.

- *Protected* means that any members following the keyword can be accessed by member functions within the same class and by member functions of classes derived from this class. For example:

```
class Access  {
   int X;       // private by default
   int Y;       // private by default
```

```
public:
  Access();   // Constructor is public and can be accessed
              // from anywhere within the same scope.

private:
  int X;      // explicitly declared private

protected:
  int A;      // can now be accessed by any class
};            // derived from Access
```

- *Friends* are functions that are given permission to access a class's private data. You declare friend functions within a class declaration, as follows:

```
class Has_friends {
  int X;              // X and Y are private by default.
   int Y;
public:
  Has_friends();
  ~Has_Friends();
  friend void Access_X_Y();
};
```

The function *Access_X_Y()* isn't one of *Has_friends'* methods, but it can access the private characteristics, *X* and *Y,* because it's a friend.

Turbo Pascal has only one access keyword: *private*. You define private methods at the end of an object after you've defined its public characteristics. Any characteristic declared after the keyword *private* can only be accessed by objects, procedures, or functions within the same unit. Objects and functions outside the unit can access the public parts of the object. Turbo Pascal has established its access firmly along the lines of units.

```
type
  Myobject = object
  Field1;    { These characteristics are public by default. }
  Field2;
  procedure Behavior1;
```

```
private
  Field3;      { This characteristic is private. }
end;
```

An object type protects data by establishing the relationships between data and methods. Data can only be accessed by methods explicitly created for accessing the data or by functions outside the type given permission to access the data. You're less likely to manipulate the wrong data with the right methods and vice versa.

When you plan and define object types thoroughly enough, users of the object won't want or need to access its characteristics directly; they'll access them by sending a message to the object, which will in turn access its own data.

Once you define an object type (a C++ class or Turbo Pascal object), anyone can use it without knowing specifically how it's implemented. Object types are the fundamental difference between object-oriented languages and traditional procedural languages.

About Types

The concept of type is essential to programming. The type of a variable tells us the range of values or states it can assume and the operators you can apply to it. Specific instances of a type have values or states determined by the operators that can manipulate them.

For example, in C++, any variable of type *int* can have a value from -32,768 to 32,767 and can be added, subtracted, multiplied, divided, compared, and so on. An integer in Turbo Pascal has the same range. A *longint* (in Turbo Pascal) or *long* (in C++) can have a value in the range -2,147,483,648 to 2,147,483,647 and can be added, multiplied, and so on.

Types come in all shapes and sizes (one byte, two bytes, four bytes, eight bytes, and so on) and are either built into the language or built from simpler types.

The built-in types in C++ are *char*, *int*, *float*, and *double*. Four specifiers — *long*, *short*, *signed*, and *unsigned* — expand these simple types into a larger set. A structured type (such as *array* or *struct*) holds more than one simple type. These and others, such as pointers, are built into the language. The compiler already knows how to handle these types and doesn't have to learn about them each time it encounters an instance of one.

Pascal has a slightly different group of built-in types that the compiler knows about in advance (*int*, *char*, *string*, *real*, and *boolean*). It too can handle these types without having to learn about them.

To define an instance of a built-in type, you simply name a variable and specify its type. (When you define a variable, you create space for it; when you declare a variable, you tell the compiler that space exists for it and what it looks like.)

You define an instance of a built-in type in C++ as follows:

```
int AnyNumber;
```

In Turbo Pascal:

```
AnyNumber : integer;
```

Declaring a composite type of built-in types is almost as simple. In C++:

```
struct Numbers {
   int X;
   double Y;
};
```

and in Turbo Pascal:

```
Numbers = record
   X : integer;
   Y: double;
end;
```

43

A type describes the general characteristics and behaviors of a group of related objects. A variable is an instance of the type. C++ and Turbo Pascal make it easy to package, extend, and use these user-defined types. This new ability encourages you to rethink how you create systems and write code.

To create your own object types, you declare the type, then define an instance of it. In C++, you can declare a class to represent the characteristics and behaviors of fruit:

```
// Enumerated types — colors and sizes;
// these can also be declared inside the class.
enum Colors {red, yellow, green, brown, orange};
enum Sizes {small, medium, large};

class AnyFruit {
  colors Color;      // private by default
  sizes Size;
public:
  void Growth_behavior();
};
```

In Turbo Pascal:

```
Colors = (red, yellow, green, brown, orange);
Sizes = ( small, medium, large);

AnyFruit = object
  Color : colors;    { public by default }
  Size : sizes;
  procedure Growth_behavior;
end;
```

You can then define a variable of the type in C++, as follows:

```
aFruit AnyFruit;
```

where the variable *aFruit* is an instance of the class *AnyFruit*. In Turbo Pascal, the declaration is:

```
AnyFruit : aFruit;
```

44

You implement classes and objects by implementing their methods, just as you implement functions in C++ and procedures and functions in Turbo Pascal.

A possible implementation of the *Growth_behavior* method in C++ is:

```
void AnyFruit :: Growth_behavior()
{
  if (size != large)              // Check enumerated values.
    size++;
};
```

and in Turbo Pascal:

```
procedure AnyFruit.Growth_behavior;
begin
  If (Size <> large) then
    Size := Size + 1;
end;
```

The compiler treats user-defined object types just like types built into the language. *Growth_behavior* already knows about *Size* (they're part of the same type, *AnyFruit*), so you don't have to pass *Size* to it.

Constructors and Destructors

When you define an instance of a built-in type, the compiler creates space for it in memory. In effect, the compiler constructs the variable. When the variable is no longer needed, the compiler releases the space it used. In other words, it destroys the variable.

To make user-defined types as similar as possible to built-in types, the compiler needs comparable construction and destruction power. With built-in types, the compiler already knows the size of each type. When you define a type, the compiler must figure out how much space to allocate and deallocate for it.

In C++ and Turbo Pascal, constructors and destructors handle initialization and cleanup. In C++, if you don't supply a constructor (or constructors — there can be more than one) and a destructor (there can only be one) for a class, the compiler automatically constructs and destructs the class the simplest way it can. If the simplest way isn't sufficient, you can define your own.

The constructor in C++ is a method with the same name as the class. The class destructor is the class name preceded by a tilde (~). The following fragment declares a class, *AnyClass*, with a constructor and destructor:

```
class AnyClass {
public:
  AnyClass;          // constructor
  ~AnyClass;         // destructor
};
```

The following declares an object with a constructor and destructor in Turbo Pascal:

```
AnyObject = object
  constructor Init;
  destructor Done;
end;

AnyObject.Init;
begin                { constructor }
end;

AnyObject.Done
begin                { destructor }
end;
```

In Turbo Pascal, you name constructors and destructors explicitly. They can be any names (not just *Init* and *Done*):

```
AnyObject = object
  constructor Setup;
  destructor Reset;
end;
```

```
{ implementation }

AnyObject.Setup;
begin
end;

AnyObject.Reset
begin
end;
```

You can also have the constructor do something with an object's characteristics. The declaration in C++ is:

```
class Gauge {
  int Temp;                    // private characteristics by default
  int Pressure;
public:
  Gauge(int Init_Temp, int Init_Pressure);    // constructor
  ~Gauge();
};
```

and the implementation:

```
Gauge::Gauge(int Init_Temp, int Init_Pressure);
  Temp = Init_temp;
  Press = Init_pressure;
};
```

The declaration in Turbo Pascal is:

```
Gauge = object
  Temp : integer;    { public by default }
  Pressure : integer;
  constructor init(Init_Temp : integer; Init_Pressure : integer);
  destructor done;
end;
```

and the implementation:

```
constructor Gauge.Init(Init_Temp : integer;
                Init_pressure : integer);
```

```
begin
  Temp := Init_temp;
  Pressure := Init_pressure;
end;
```

The Importance of Being Constructed

Turbo Pascal programmers take note: Since the addresses of methods in the VMT are initialized in the constructor call, it's absolutely critical that you call a constructor before attempting to use any methods in an object that has virtual methods. It's good programming practice to write a constructor, even if you don't initially need virtual methods. If you forget to write and call a constructor in an object that has virtual methods and then make a method call with the object, the table will contain garbage addresses and your program will most likely lock up.

You can't achieve the same level of privacy in Turbo Pascal as in C++ (even by using the Turbo Pascal keyword *private*) without some very restrictive coding. That means declaring private characteristics and putting only one type in a unit:

```
Gauge = object
  constructor init(Init_Temp : integer; Init_Pressure : integer);
  destructor done;
private:
  Temp : integer;    { private; only accessible from this unit }
  Pressure : integer;
end;
```

In Turbo Pascal, you must explicitly declare a constructor if you use virtual methods and a destructor if you intend to create dynamic objects. Because a static object's memory requirements are known at compile time, however, constructors and destructors are unnecessary. Turbo Pascal is picky about construction and destruction and requires that you call the constructor and destructor yourself. C++ calls them for you and, if you haven't declared any, will call a default constructor and destructor for you.

Don't get the wrong impression; I'm not recommending one language over the other. Their distinctive implementations of object-oriented features emphasize one of the important themes of the Tao of objects: that object-oriented programming is an evolving, dynamic vision of what a programming language should be. If you're already using Pascal or C, the "best" language for learning object-oriented programming is one that builds on what you know.

Messages

Conventional programming systems typically view a program as a collection of procedures. Procedures are the active components; data is passive. If we declare data globally, any procedure can get at it and the likelihood of incorrect data manipulation is high.

If we declare data locally (within a procedure), only that procedure can access it; the data is safer, but it's overly restricted. What's needed is more flexibility so that data can be accessed by any number of defined procedures. In object-oriented programming, a method knows which data it can manipulate, and data knows which methods can manipulate it.

In a procedural program, the flow of control is determined by the ordering of procedures and control mechanisms, such as *if*, *while*, *switch*, and so on. This implies that we know how to structure the entire program during program creation. In programs designed to capture the essence of a dynamic world, this assumption is unrealistic. The world is changing, and our ideas and models of the world must adapt. A better alternative captures the design flow in terms of logical relationships among objects.

Object-oriented programming captures these logical relationships in objects, and the flow of control in an object-oriented program is determined by the messages sent to objects. When you send a message, you clarify the communication among the components of a program. Objects respond to the messages sent to them and can send messages to other objects.

The term *message* is somewhat unfortunate since it's easily confused with *method* and seems to imply that operations take place asynchronously (like broadcast messages on a network or phone messages in an office). In fact, messages are implemented as indirect function calls and thus take place immediately, just like a traditional function call.

Messages, rather than data, move around the system. Instead of saying "invoke a function on a piece of data" (the procedural approach), you say "send a message to an object" (the object-oriented approach). To send a message to an object, you specify the object and the method you want to invoke.

Let's say you've declared the following *Point* type in C++:

```
class Point {
  int X;
  int Y;
public:
  int state;
  Point(int InitX, int InitY);        // constructor
  int IsVisible();                     // Is point on or off?
};                                     // Return state.
```

Point's characteristics are its location on the screen (X and Y coordinates). Its behaviors are to construct itself and to say whether or not it's visible.

You can define an instance of *Point* and initialize it at the same time using *Point*'s constructor:

```
int Visible;
Visible = Point ThisPoint(5,10); // Define/initialize ThisPoint.
```

You can then ask *ThisPoint* if it's visible by sending it a message:

```
ThisPoint.IsVisible();
```

You can define a similar *Point* type in Turbo Pascal:

```
Point = object
  X : integer;
```

```
  Y : integer;
  State : integer;
  constructor init(InitX, InitY : integer);
  function IsVisible: integer;    { Is the point on or off? }
                                  { Return state. }
end;
```

In Turbo Pascal, you use two lines of code to first declare the *Point* object and then initialize it by calling the constructor:

```
var

ThisPoint : Point;

begin
  ThisPoint.Init(5,10);
end;
```

You can ask *ThisPoint* if it's visible by sending it a message:

```
var
  Visible : integer;

begin
  Visible := ThisPoint.IsVisible;
end;
```

Sending a message means calling an object's method, which manipulates or interprets the type's characteristics. In other words, if you want something done, you send a message to an instance of an object type, and the object handles it. Sending messages is a crucial aspect of object-oriented programming.

In this chapter I've introduced some of the concepts of object-oriented programming, the most important being the three cornerstones: encapsulation, inheritance, and polymorphism. These are the building blocks that will be used in the following chapters as you learn more about the details of object-oriented programming through examples and ideas.

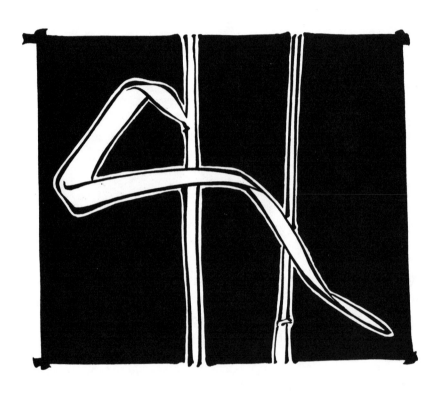

CHAPTER 2

Thinking in Objects

The world is formed from the void, like utensils from a block of wood.
The master knows the utensils, yet keeps to the block: thus he can use
all things.

In the practice of the Tao, every day something is dropped.
—Lao-tzu

The ability to create user-defined types helps clarify relationships between data and operations, between distinct blocks of code, and between the world and our programming model of the world.

Objects are more powerful than units and modules because you can create and destroy instances of a type at run time. Real-world events are dynamic, and systems that model or simulate real-world events require that types be created and destroyed on the fly.

While most programming languages treat programs (and the modules or units that compose them) as static entities, object-oriented languages let programs anticipate change, both in themselves and in the world they model. A user-defined type can do anything a module can (and considerably more).

A big problem, even if you agree that objects are useful, is envisioning them. What should go into an object? What should its boundaries be? Should the object be big or small? More or less general? And how restrictive? Should it expect to change? We'll get to all these questions as we begin describing a system for designing and building objects.

You write programs to answer questions about the world outside the program, to interact with that world, or to create tools that help you model or understand that world. Since the world you're modeling already consists of objects, you can organize object-oriented programs around representations of these objects.

For fun (one of the best reasons I can think of to program), and to get you thinking in objects, let's look at a few of the many objects in the real and computing worlds. We'll just describe (or prototype) things without concerning ourselves with the objects' implementation details.

One interesting design implication of object-oriented programming is that you can sketch out a system and delay writing the implementation code. You can see if things work at the earliest possible moment (in other words, that your code compiles) without linking in all the modules that use the interface. This saves time and encourages you to experiment rather than become locked into ideas. And if you plan your interface well, you can isolate the code you need to change and isolate errors in code.

How would you represent a simple object like a clock? Let's say it consists of the characteristics *current_time*, *current_date*, and *alarm_time* and the behaviors *tick* (the mechanism for running the clock) and *get_alarm_status*. You could describe it like this in C++:

```
class clock {
  int current_time;
  int current_date;
  int alarm_time;
public:
  clock();     // Initialize current time, date, and alarm to 0.
  int get_alarm_status(); // Return 1 if alarm is on.
  void tick();
};
```

and like this in Turbo Pascal:

```
Clock = object
  Current_time : integer;
  Current_date : integer;
  Alarm_time : integer;
  constructor init;
  destructor done;
  function get_alarm_status: integer;
  procedure tick;
end;
```

Or how about an object type to describe the clothing worn by a fashion model? In C++:

```
char underwear[12];
char shirt[15];
char socks[8];
enum Clothes (underwear, shirt, socks);

class Fashion_Model{
  his_underwear underwear; // private by default
public:
  his_shirt shirt;         // public by declaration
protected:
  his_socks socks;         // protected by declaration
};
```

In Turbo Pascal:

```
var

Underwear : string[12];
Shirt : string [15];
Socks : string [8];

type

Clothes = (Underwear, Shirt, Socks);

Fashion_Model = object
```

```
  Shirt : His_shirt;                 { public by default }
  Socks : His_socks;
private
  Underwear : His_underwear;         { private to unit by definition }
end;
```

How about a window? Not the one you're looking out of now, but one on your gloriously colored VGA screen. Let's define one consisting of dimensions, a title box, a border state, and a way to change the border state. In C++:

```
class Window {
  int X1;            // upper left
  int Y1;            // upper left
  int X2;            // bottom right
  int Y2;            // bottom right
  char Title[40];
  int border state;
public:
  void change_border_state();
};
```

In Turbo Pascal:

```
Window = object
  X1 : integer; (* upper left *)
  Y1 : integer; (* upper left *)
  X2 : integer; (* upper right *)
  Y2 : integer; (* upper right *)
  Title : string[40];
  Border_state : integer;
  procedure Change_border_state;
end;
```

Don't fret that the window is too simple. Part of the beauty of object-oriented programming is that it lets you extend objects without penalty. If you want to create a fancier window, skip ahead to Chapter 3 and derive it from this one.

The first way you should think about objects is in small, simple chunks. The second way is to think generally by imagining the fundamental concepts, characteristics, and behaviors of objects.

Consider a buffer, in this case a structure for holding *char*s or strings. Give it the characteristics *size*, *front*, and *rear* and a constructor to initialize the buffer. In C++:

```
class Buffer {
  char buf[256];
  int size;
  int front;
  int rear;
public:
  Buffer()          // constructor to init Buffer
  ~Buffer();        // destructor
};
```

The constructor initializes the buffer by setting each *char* to 0. In C++:

```
Buffer::Buffer() {
int count;
for (count = 0; count < 257; buf[count] = 0; count++);
};
```

In Turbo Pascal:

```
Buffer = object
  Buf     :  string[256];
  Size    :  integer;
  Front   :  integer;
  Rear    :  integer;
  constructor init;
  destructor done;
end;
```

The constructor implementation is:

```
constructor Buffer.Init;
var
  Count : integer;
begin
  For Count := 1 to 256 do
    Buf[Count] := 0;
end;
```

This simple buffer might not be what you had in mind. You might want to add and delete items from the buffer, for example. Don't worry about it; you can add the parts you need as you go along. When you first imagine an object, think of it only as an experiment, a start. Object-oriented programming encourages this kind of thinking.

Imagine you need to simulate the activity of a group of teachers to come up with an efficient schedule for a school. You can think of teachers as objects and describe them accordingly, in terms of the behavior that affects the school's schedule. You might need to know what their free periods are, which subjects they can teach, how they teach, and so on. You could represent a teacher as follows in C++:

```
enum Subjects {music, English, physics, biology, calculus}

class Teacher {
   int FreePeriod;
   subjects Subject;
public:
   Teacher();              // Construct a teacher.
   ~Teacher();             // Destroy a teacher.
   void Teaching_Behavior();
};
```

In Turbo Pascal:

```
Subjects = (music, English, physics, biology, calculus);

Teacher = object
   FreePeriod: int;
   Subject : subjects;
   constructor init;
   destructor done;
   procedure Teaching_behavior();
end;
```

You might then build a complete scheduling system out of a group of objects: teacher, students, school, and so forth. There might be different types of teachers, each inheriting from the abstract type shown above.

Complex Numbers

A complex number represents a point on a plane. You can represent this point using either Cartesian (an X,Y pair) or polar coordinates (an angle from an axis and a distance), as shown in Figures 2-1 and 2-2. A type for manipulating complex numbers might consist of methods for returning the values of X and Y (the Cartesian representation), returning the distance and an angle (the polar representation), adding complex numbers, and so on.

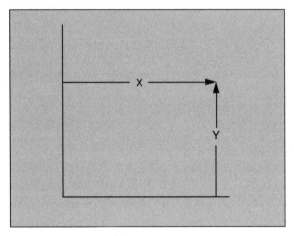

Figure 2-1. Cartesian coordinates.

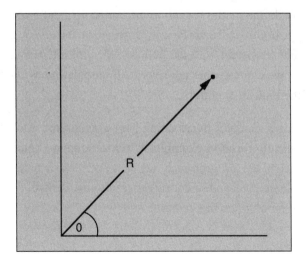

Figure 2-2. Polar coordinates.

Here's one possible declaration in C++:

```
class Complex {
  float X, Y, Distance, Angle;
public:
  float FindX();                // Return X.
  float FindY();                // Return Y.
  float FindDistance();         // Return Distance.
  float FindAngle();            // Return Angle.
  float Add();                  // Return sum.
};
```

In Turbo Pascal:

```
Complex = object
  X, Y, Distance, Angle : real;
  function FindX : real;
  function FindY : real;
  function FindDistance : real;
  function FindAngle : real;
  function Add: real;           { Return sum. }
end;
```

Operator Overloading in C++

We can easily define methods such as *add*, *subtract*, and so on for a complex number object type in C++ or Turbo Pascal. However, using *add* or *subtract* in place of + or - isn't quite consistent with the built-in types for integers or floating-point numbers. In C++, we can use operator overloading to define methods that are the same as any of the built-in operators.

Strictly speaking, operator overloading isn't a requirement in object-oriented programming; rather, it's another example of "syntactic sugar" since it makes things look more like what the programmer has in mind. It's a nice touch, though, particularly in mathematical and scientific programming. Perhaps future versions of Turbo Pascal will incorporate this feature.

Types, Not Individuals

It's important to realize that you're interested less in individual objects than in types of objects. When you create a type, you need to imagine not the specific case, but the general case. If you're modeling a system that needs to describe employees, create a type that represents the general class of employees and go from there, creating instances and deriving subtypes.

In C++:

```
class employee {
  char last_name [28];
  char first_name [15];
  double employee_id;
  double SS_number;
  float salary;
  void do_job();
};
```

In Turbo Pascal:

```
Employee = Object
  Last_name : string[28];
  First_name : string[15];
  Employee_id : double;
  SS_number : double;
  Salary : real;
  procedure do_job;
end;
```

An individual of the *employee* type is an instance of *employee*. In C++:

```
employee AnEmployee;
```

In Turbo Pascal:

```
AnEmployee : Employee;
```

Let's go a step further and outline a few simple rules for creating object types. We'll assume the object types you create will share the following characteristics:

- They might need to be extended.

- Methods within the object might be customized, overridden, or reimplemented by descendants.

- You might want to create instances of these types at run time.

- The types exist within a system, which will likely grow into a hierarchy of types.

If this is the case, you want to decide at least a few things as early as possible. The most important of these is the interface or protocol for the object types that will compose the hierarchy.

How Complex Should Objects Be?

When you define objects, it's important to balance functionality and reusability. Resist the urge to create large "kitchen-sink" objects that do everything. Unfortunately, this kind of object suffers from being hard to understand and, worse, hard to reuse. Instead, try to create objects that have a single, well-defined purpose. Rather than creating a complex application (such as an integrated spreadsheet, database, word processor, and video game), break one or two main objects down according to their basic functionality.

You'll find that these objects, in turn, are composed of simpler objects, each dedicated to a single purpose. For example, the word-processor object might be broken down into a text-buffer object, a formatter, a printer, a window, a menu, and so on.

When you break objects down into simple ones, you'll find that your programs are easier to understand and maintain. They can also be smaller because of the high degree of reusability. If you start creating objects that can't be explained in a few sentences or have more than 50 or 60 methods, it's time to break things down into smaller pieces.

You'll also find that the pieces you write tend to be smaller when you use object-oriented techniques. If you're used to writing 100- to 200-line functions or procedures, you may find that your methods are much shorter, perhaps 30 to 40 lines of object-oriented code. This is because each message can do more and because you want to program with a finer level of granularity. In the pure object-oriented languages, it's not uncommon to find very useful methods consisting of fewer than 10 lines.

Base and Abstract Types

A base type defines a common interface to a group of similar types. It generalizes the intended uses for a hierarchy of types. In other words, it describes the range of messages, or protocol, an object of a type can respond to.

Object-oriented programming clearly distinguishes the interface from the implementation. The interface in C++ is the class declaration; in Turbo Pascal, it's the object definition. The interface says "here's what a type looks like, and here are its behaviors." It doesn't specify how the type behaves; it leaves that to the implementation.

The interface must be visible everywhere an object type is used. The implementation must be in only one spot. From a design perspective, this allows you to prototype code (via the interface) without implementing it and therefore reduce errors, since you can modify the implementation without disturbing the interface.

A base type can be simple. In C++:

```
class Base {
public:
  Base();
  ~Base();
};
```

In Turbo Pascal:

```
Base = object
  constructor init;
  destructor done;
end;
```

A base type can also be more complex. In C++:

```
class Base {
  int Some_characteristic;
public:
  Base();
  ~Base();
  void Behavior1();
  void Behavior2();
  void Behavior3();        // and so on
};
```

In Turbo Pascal:

```
Base = object
  Some_characteristic : integer;
  constructor init;
  destructor done;
  procedure Behavior1;
  procedure Behavior2;
  procedure Behavior3;
end;
```

An object type is, in itself, a very useful concept. However, object types aren't restricted to working in isolation. Just as you think of types in the world as hierarchies (an aspen is a type of tree, a type of plant, and a type of living entity), you can treat types in object-oriented programming as hierarchies. From a hierarchical perspective, a base type is a node in the hierarchy and can itself be a derived type.

Base can be the head of a hierarchy:

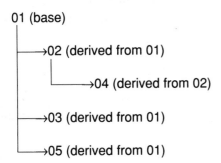

01 (base)

    →02 (derived from 01)

        →04 (derived from 02)

    →03 (derived from 01)

    →05 (derived from 01)

a node in a hierarchy:

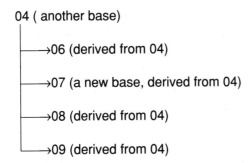

04 (another base)

    →06 (derived from 04)

    →07 (a new base, derived from 04)

    →08 (derived from 04)

    →09 (derived from 04)

and subsequently a *Base* for another hierarchy:

07 (another base)

    →10 (derived from 07)

    →11 (derived from 07)

    →12 (derived from 07)

A particular kind of base type called an *abstract type* is used strictly for creating other object types. An abstract type has no instances and thus is normally used to derive new types. It specifies an interface for all types derived from it. Abstract types are the pathways to extending an object-oriented system.

C++ explicitly supports abstract classes via the pure virtual function. The keyword *virtual* is important in object-oriented programming, one we'll be using in many examples. We'll discuss the use of *virtual* in more detail later, but for now think of it in terms of early and late binding.

When you call a statically bound method, the compiler figures out at compile time exactly which function to call. Static (or early) binding means the compiler allocates and resolves all references to functions at compile time. In an object-oriented system, you want to send a message to an object and let the object decide how to respond.

You're asking the compiler to resolve some references at run time (late or dynamic binding). To resolve references to methods at run time, you create virtual methods. These allow derived types to have their own versions of a base-type method.

In C++, you specify that a virtual function is pure by assigning its definition to zero:

```
class abstract {
//...
public:
  abstract()
  virtual void behavior() = 0;
//...
};
```

Turbo Pascal doesn't allow explicit assignment during the interface. To declare an abstract object in Turbo Pascal, describe its interface and make its definition empty:

```
Abstract = object
  constructor init;
  destructor done;
  virtual procedure Behavior;
end;
```

Its implementation is:

```
procedure Abstract.Behavior;
begin
end;
```

You can alternatively use the standard procedure, *Abstract*, when implementing an abstract object type. This will ensure that attempts to use instances of the abstract type will cause a run-time error.

An abstract class supports the idea of generality. The classic example of an abstract class is a shape, which might consist of concrete variants such as ellipse, circle, rectangle, triangle, and so on. By definition, an abstract class in C++ can only be used as a base class of some other class.

If you use abstract object types, you can change the interface and immediately propagate changes throughout the system. All changes to the abstract type are retroactive through its derived types.

Abstract vs. Concrete

No formal language distinction exists between how you declare abstract data types and how you declare "concrete" or derived objects. Instead, the difference is found at the implementation level in how they are defined and used. Abstract types, by their nature, usually aren't fully complete; they tend to have some abstract methods that are implemented only in descendant types. Nonetheless, abstract types are the key to providing reusable objects.

You should always try to solve general problems and therefore come up with generic, reusable abstract types, then create derived types that solve the specific problem at hand. This will ensure that you have some reusable objects for similar problems. You can also have several layers of abstract types that build on each other, each becoming a bit more concrete, a bit more problem-specific, as you move down the hierarchy.

One clear distinction between abstract and more concrete types is that abstract types serve only to gather common code; you never create objects of the abstract types, except for testing. Instead, you create descendants of the abstract types. When creating abstract types, be careful to document completely the public protocol used in descendants.

Planning for Change

A system developed using object-oriented techniques allows you to reuse and extend code you didn't write without having access to source code. The only requirement is that the designers and coders of the classes you want to reuse planned for change by creating abstract classes, creating classes that are general enough to allow themselves to be extended, and using virtual methods.

When defining your own object types, you should consider how your types relate to the types they model in the real world and how reusable they are. For example, the following code segment creates an abstract user-defined type (called *AnyClass* in C++ and *AnyObject* in Turbo Pascal) that contains a virtual abstract *AnyBehavior* method. This method allows any class or object derived from *AnyClass* or *AnyObject* to create its own *AnyBehavior* method.

In C++ :

```
class AnyClass {
public:
  AnyClass;                     // constructor
  ~AnyClass;                    // destructor
  virtual void AnyBehavior() = 0;
};
```

In Turbo Pascal:

```
AnyObject = object
   constructor init;
   destructor done;
   virtual procedure AnyBehavior;
end;
```

You don't know how any future types derived from *AnyClass* or *AnyObject* will implement *AnyBehavior*. *AnyClass* and *AnyObject* are generalizations and thus can easily be extended to create any number of specific types and behaviors. Classes and objects built up this way (from abstract, extensible types) can be distributed in libraries that can themselves be extended, even without access to the library's source code, through inheritance. To extend the library, you simply derive a new object type and reimplement its virtual behaviors.

The Trickle-Up Theory

You'll find that your first attempts at creating reusable abstract types aren't very successful. A method here or there is missing, and you end up implementing something in the derived object type. If you create another derived type, you may find yourself writing almost the same code. With some careful attention to these situations, you'll be able to make these two methods more general-purpose and move them up to the base type.

This is what I call the "trickle-up theory." It says that as you implement new descendant types, you often find some of the functionality moving up into the base type, where it can also be inherited by other derived types. This happens to even the most experienced object-oriented programmers and is part of the dynamic evolution of object types.

Until you've successfully reused base objects two or three times with new derived types, you'll find that some changes are required. But if you keep at it, you'll become better at solving general problems and will eventually create abstract types almost instinctively.

Brad Cox, designer of the object-oriented programming language Objective-C, coined the phrase "the software IC" to refer to objects that are completely encapsulated and reusable. Just as in the hardware world, our goal is to create reusable components that are "plug-compatible" with each other. That way, you can substitute different objects that implement the same protocol as your programs respond to the changing needs of users.

Objects, Classes, and Types

Objects are all around us. They help us learn, remember, and organize our lives. We group the world (often subconsciously) into related object types.

For example, dogs represent a template for a group of dogs with similar characteristics and behaviors. *Malamute*, *Labrador Retriever*, and *German Shepherd* are subtypes of the type *Dog*. My dog Luke is an instance of the subclass *Labrador Retriever* of class *Dog*.

Font is a name we use to depict the size and shape of characters. It's a type (no pun intended) that can consist of many subtypes, such as *Courier*, *Prestige*, *Tiffany*, and so on. The list of types (classes or objects) goes on and on.

This book is a plan for anticipating growth and change in the world in which you live and work. A common pitfall of procedural systems is what is sometimes called "the one-function solution": You assume you're writing code as if there's only one instance of a problem. The solution is hard-wired into the system. When faced with a slightly different problem later, you have to redesign the system. Not a good approach.

When you create a new object type, you're extending the abilities of the language. And by establishing an interface to a group of types, you open the door for the sensible development of huge projects. This interface can remain the same even if you later improve the implementation, so you can modify code without affecting the rest of the system.

The interface of a type is enforced by the compiler, not by a person or a set of guidelines. This makes the integration of types into the final product much easier and simpler. The compiler enforces the proper use of the type, ensures the proper initialization and cleanup of objects, and verifies that message passing is performed properly.

Object-oriented programming offers the best techniques I know of for anticipating and incorporating change in program development.

It's as easy to create a type as it is to create an individual — almost. And once you've created a type, you can generate an entire system of types from it through inheritance.

Although many of the benefits of encapsulation are convenient for small programming projects, encapsulation is particularly valuable when you begin to "program in the large." It helps you build programs more quickly and easily.

Many languages can easily handle small- to medium-sized programs; the problems crop up when the programs get really big. C and Pascal, with extensions for separate compilation, allow programming in the large, but little nuisances of the languages become tremendous liabilities when you're creating large programs. They can easily bring a project to its knees.

The little inconveniences become very important as the system grows. C++ and Turbo Pascal, by supporting encapsulation and the rules associated with the new data types, remove many of the problems that prevent programming in the large. This means not only that a big team working on a big project can easily construct and integrate the system, but that a small team or a single person, using predefined types created for earlier projects or distributed by vendors, can build and maintain systems they previously couldn't have conceived of. This opens up amazing possibilities for creativity.

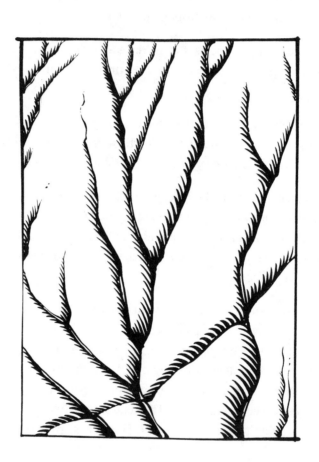

CHAPTER 3

Extending the System

*To find the origin, trace back the manifestations. When you recognize
the children, and find the mother, you'll be free of sorrow.*
                                        — Lao-tzu

*Like modern physicists, Buddhists see all objects as processes in a
universal flux, and deny the existence of any material substance.*
                                        — Fritjof Capra

We learn about, use, and organize objects in the world by classifying them into
general and specific types based on similarities and differences in states and
behaviors. For example, mandolins, fiddles, banjos, and guitars are all types of
stringed musical instruments. Their common behaviors are that they can be played
and that playing them makes music. Their common state is whether they're being
played.

The way you play each instrument depends on its characteristics. One characteristic is the number of strings. A mandolin has eight strings, a fiddle four, a banjo
four or five, and a guitar four, six, or 12. *Mandolin, fiddle, banjo,* and *guitar* are specific types of the general type *stringed musical instrument.* In object-oriented programming, we express this kind of specification with inheritance.

Through inheritance, an object type inherits all the characteristics of an existing
type and adds some specific characteristics or behaviors of its own. Examples of
inheritance are common. In the programming world, for example, you can organize
languages by classifying them into a base type and specific types derived from it.
Figure 3-1 shows how you might do that. Beginning with a general type (*language*),
you could derive the specific types (*functional, imperative,* and *logical*) and the more
specific types (*C, Pascal, LISP, Prolog, C++, Turbo Pascal,* and *Prolog++*).

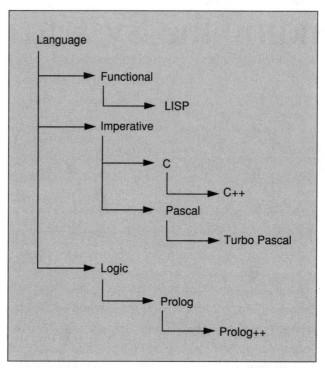

Figure 3-1. Beginning with a general type (*Language*), you can derive specific types.

In this scenario, *C* and *Pascal* are derived from *imperative* and thus have features in common with all imperative languages. *C++* is derived, in turn, from *C*. And *Turbo Pascal* is derived from *Pascal*. *C++* and *Turbo Pascal* are *extended*: imperative languages with object-oriented extensions.

The simplest way to extend a system is to add new features to an existing type. In the language hierarchy, *Prolog* is a type of logic language. *Prolog++* is a type of *Prolog*, extended by the addition of object-oriented features. Extension in this case is mostly organizational.

In a more complex scenario, you extend a system by adding subtypes to it without disrupting outside control of the system.

Imagine a system consisting of functions for controlling related shapes (Figure 3-2). Using object-oriented techniques, you can add a new shape to the system without changing the shape controller (Figure 3-3).

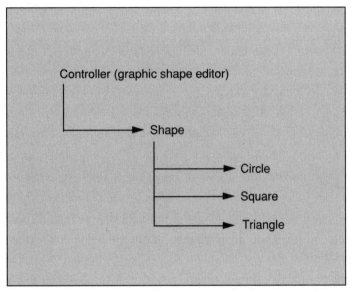

Figure 3-2. A system consisting of functions for controlling related shapes.

The controller (in this case, a graphic shape editor) already knows how to handle shapes, so it will know how to handle new ones derived from the base shape. The controller sends the same message (say, *display*) to any of the shapes, and each shape figures out how to display itself. We call this *polymorphism*.

Imagine an air traffic controller system that directs traffic in a metropolitan airport (Figure 3-4). You can add a new type of flying object (a flying saucer, for example) without modifying the air traffic controller (Figure 3-5).

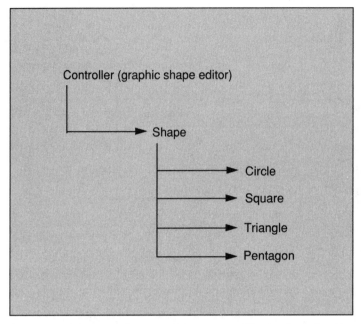

Figure 3-3. You can add a new shape to the system without changing the shape controller.

Once you've defined a new base type, you can build on it using inheritance. When a new type inherits from a base type, the derived type gets all the characteristics and behaviors of the base type.

Inheritance allow you to reuse code without introducing bugs. Let's say you've created a base type in C++:

```
class base {
   int state1;
   int state2;
public:
   void Behavior();
};
```

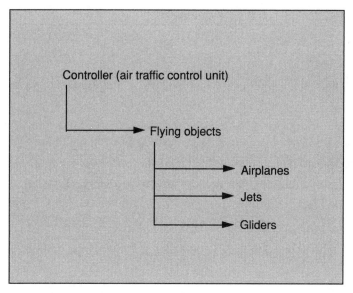

Figure 3-4. Air traffic controller system.

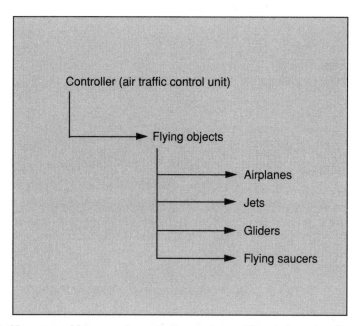

Figure 3-5. You can add a new shape to the system without changing the shape controller.

77

or in Turbo Pascal:

```
base = object
  State1 : integer;
  State2 : integer;
  procedure Behavior;
end;
```

Now you want to build a new type derived from the existing base type. The derived type should be identical to the base type, with one exception: You want to extend *base* by adding a second method, called *Behavior2*. You can build *derived* simply and quickly by inheriting from *base*. You don't recode anything in the derived type that you want to keep from the base type; you just add the new behavior.

In C++:

```
class derived : public base {
public:
  void Behavior2();
};
```

In Turbo Pascal:

```
derived = object (base)
  procedure Behavior2;
end;
```

Since *derived* inherits all the data and methods of *base*, you don't need to redefine them. You simply tell the compiler you want to derive a new type (*derived*) from a base type (*base*) and add the new method.

Now you can send either message (*Behavior1* or *Behavior2*) to variables of the derived type, and *derived* can handle it. In C++:

```
main() {
  derived d;
  d.state1 = 1984;
  d.state2 = 1992;
  d.behavior1();
  d.behavior2();
}
```

In Turbo Pascal:

```
var
d: derived;
With d do
  begin
    State1:= 1984;
    State2:= 1992;
    Behavior1;
    Behavior2;
  end;
```

Notice again that you don't have to pass the variables *State1* and *State2* to *Behavior2*; *derived* inherited knowledge of them from *base*.

Sketching Your Objects

Although there's no formal methodology for object-oriented design, one of the most important steps when you begin is to make sure you understand the objects you're creating. You can do this by sketching out the data and functionality for each thing you think will be an object. Just write down the data fields and methods for each type on paper or index cards. Don't worry about the low-level details of how the fields or methods are implemented; concentrate on the high-level view. If some functionality is related to the data, it may be that you only need a *struct* or *record* instead of an object. In a hybrid language, there's nothing wrong with that.

As you sketch out the objects, try to draw upon the real-world system you're modeling, whether it's a business system, scientific application, or whatever. If there aren't any real-world components to start with, as with some of the examples presented later in this chapter, you can abstract them based on the user interface. For example, what kinds of windows will there be? What does each window contain? Similarly, you'll want to break down the more complex objects into their own objects, which also consist of data and methods.

When you create your list of objects, don't worry too much about the inheritance structure. It's much easier to list the objects on index cards and then see which have duplicate fields or methods. One advantage of using index cards is that you can move them around to try out different approaches to creating hierarchies. Remember that inheritance should only be used when you inherit both the data and the functionality. In many cases, you'll want to use composition so that some objects are contained in others.

Reusing Code

Inheritance encourages the reuse of code, which saves time and makes code maintenance easier. In addition, inheritance lets you use and extend code you didn't write — even if you don't have access to the source code — and write extensible libraries that you can pass on to others without releasing source code. You can do this by:

- Creating abstract types
- Creating types that are general enough to allow themselves to be extended
- Using virtual methods
- Clearly defining an interface to these types.

The separation of interface and implementation is especially important in object-oriented programming. The interface says what the class does; the implementation says how the class works. You can compile a program using only the interface, but you can't link it. You can find out how a system works, vary the implementation as often as you like, and link it in without recompiling the entire project. This lets you extend the system by deriving related types and not disrupt the working system. It also lets you describe and compile a system (prototype it) without actually writing an implementation. You can experiment with design and implementation and not pay too much for that experimentation.

In this chapter, you'll learn how to use encapsulation and inheritance to describe systems in types that represent aspects of the world and develop a modeling system that you can use as a blueprint. This system will show how types make it easier to model real-world problems, describe a particularly interesting (and universal) aspect of the world, called *chaos*, and show the peculiar order you can discover in chaos through strange attractors.

Choosing a First Application

The best way to learn object-oriented programming is to try it. For your first project, pick a new programming task rather than reimplementing a program you've written using a traditional approach. If you reimplement a known program, you probably won't be pushed to explore the relationships between the objects and will revert to traditional techniques rather than using encapsulation, inheritance, and polymorphism. Instead, try to pick a small but new problem. Ideally, it should map to a model found in the real world, where the objects aren't too abstract.

For example, you might choose to implement a game (such as chess or checkers), a simulation (a hardware simulation of a CPU or something more abstract, like different types of fractal curves), or a simple business application (such as a calculator, spreadsheet, or project manager). If the application models the real world, you have a starting point for determining what the objects should be. Throughout the rest of this book I'll present sketches of applications that would make good first or second projects.

Checkers and Chess

Consider two board games, checkers and chess. Each game consists of related characteristics: an eight-by-eight-square board, two sets of playing pieces, rules for moving pieces, and rules for determining the end of the game. Since the games have so much in common, you can use an abstract type to create a common interface to a group of related subtypes.

Your approach might be to start with the smallest unit (a board piece) and work your way up. What are its characteristics? A board piece has a position, a set of legal moves, and a set of possible moves. To determine the legal and possible moves, we use a method.

In C++, an abstract board piece might look like this:

```
class BoardPiece {
    int X;                  // position along X axis
    int Y;                  // position along Y axis
public:
    BoardPiece();           // Construct a board piece.
    ~BoardPiece();          // Destruct a board piece.
    virtual void Legal_moves(); {}
    virtual void Possible_moves(); {}
};
```

and like this in Turbo Pascal:

```
BoardPiece = object
    X : integer;            { position along X axis }
    Y : integer;            { position along Y axis }
    construct Init;         { Construct a board piece. }
    destructor Done;        { Destruct a board piece. }
    procedure Legal_moves; virtual;
    procedure Possible_moves; virtual;
end;

Procedure Legal_moves;
begin                       { abstract }
end;
```

```
Procedure Possible_moves;
begin                           { abstract }
end;
```

Notice that the behaviors are abstract and thus are reimplemented by the types derived from *BoardPiece*. In C++, you can use the in-line feature to implement default code. The code between the braces does nothing, but by declaring the behaviors in the abstract type you emphasize that each derived type must implement its own *Legal_moves* and *Possible_moves* behaviors. Turbo Pascal has no in-line feature, so you must implement all methods (including abstract ones) separately from the declaration.

Each board piece has a position (X,Y) on the board and a way to determine its legal and possible moves. In checkers, a piece is a pawn or a king. In chess, a piece is a pawn, knight, bishop, rook, queen, or king. In both games, the pieces are related but have different legal and possible moves. By beginning with a generic *BoardPiece*, you can derive each piece without reimplementing the basic piece code. In C++, you can derive a checker pawn from the base type *BoardPiece*:

```
class CheckerPawn : public BoardPiece {
public:
  CheckerPawn();            // Construct a checker.
  ~CheckerPawn();           // Destruct a checker.
  void Legal_moves();       // Implement pawn's legal moves.
  void Possible_moves();    // Determine possible moves.
};
```

In Turbo Pascal:

```
CheckerPawn = object (BoardPiece)
  construct Init;
  destructor Done;
  procedure Legal_moves; virtual;
  procedure Possible_moves; virtual;
end;
```

You can reimplement *Legal_moves* as follows in C++:

```
CheckerPawn:: Legal_moves()
{   // Implement here.
}
```

In Turbo Pascal:

```
CheckerPawn.Legal_moves;
begin
  { Implement here. }
end;
```

CheckerKing is another board piece that reimplements *Legal_moves* and *Possible_moves*. In C++:

```
class CheckerKing : public BoardPiece {
public:
  CheckerKing();         // Construct a king.
  ~CheckerKing();        // Destruct a king.
  void Legal_moves();    // Implement king's legal moves.
  void Possible_moves(); // Determine possible moves.
};
```

In Turbo Pascal:

```
CheckerKing = object (BoardPiece)
  construct Init;
  destructor Done;
  procedure Legal_moves; virtual;
  procedure Possible_moves; virtual;
end;
```

A chess piece (a knight, for example) is just another board piece with reimplemented behaviors. In C++:

```
class Knight : public BoardPiece {
public:
  Knight();                 // Construct a knight.
```

```
  ~Knight();              // Destruct a knight.
  void Legal_moves();     // Implement legal moves.
  void Possible_moves();  // Determine possible moves.
};
```

In Turbo Pascal:

```
Knight = object (BoardPiece)
  construct Init;
  destructor Done;
  procedure Legal_moves; virtual;
  procedure Possible_moves; virtual;
end;
```

Note: Once you declare a method as virtual in C++, it remains virtual through any derived classes. Turbo Pascal requires that the keyword *virtual* be repeated every time you redeclare the method. If you don't, the compiler will behave unpredictably… but always incorrectly.

As systems become more complex, the need to derive new types and reimplement the behaviors of types becomes more noticeable and important. Object-oriented programming's strength lies in letting you extend parts of a system without reimplementing the rest.

In the game example, we derived new related types — a simple hierarchical extension. In the shapes and traffic-controller examples, we extended the system by deriving new types without disrupting the mechanism for controlling the types.

In the next section, we'll use these ideas to develop an extensible modeling system from which we can derive a variety of models.

Black Art

Modeling is a black art, a way to encapsulate part of the real world in terms of the mathematical relationships among variables. You select the variables you think are important in determining changes of state in the system, then stand back and watch the action.

For example, in a two-dimensional system with variables X and Y, we might say that the current state of Y is equal to twice the current state of X (in mathematical terms, Y = 2X). In a simple linear model like this one, you can easily visualize how the system will change from state to state: Y is always twice as big as X (Figure 3-6).

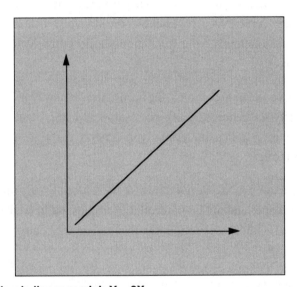

Figure 3-6. A simple linear model: Y = 2X.

In recent years, researchers in various fields that involve dynamics have used computers to model nonlinear systems. Because the parameters don't vary proportionally, these systems' behavior is not easily visualized or understood just by looking at numbers. The key to understanding many of these systems is to discover and study their attractors.

An attractor is, loosely, a state toward which a system evolves. You study attractors by looking at their pictures in a computer-generated phase, or *state*, space. In state space, a point represents all the information known about a system's state, and the space itself is a picture of the system's current state plotted against its next state (Figure 3-7).

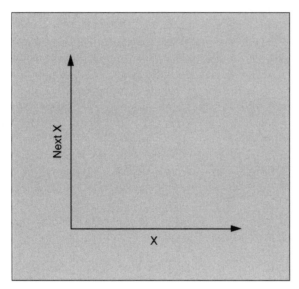

Figure 3-7. State space.

You want to know how the system is evolving or which state it's evolving toward. Attractors "attract" a system. As the system evolves (changes state), the collection of points representing successive states can either settle to one point (a point attractor; see Figure 3-8), repeatedly return to a group of points (a periodic attractor; see Figure 3-9), or not return to a clearly defined group of points (possibly strange; see Figure 3-10).

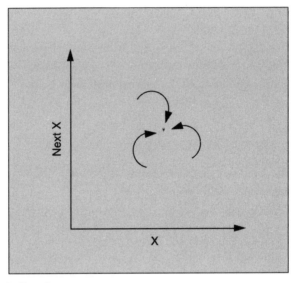

Figure 3-8. Point attractor.

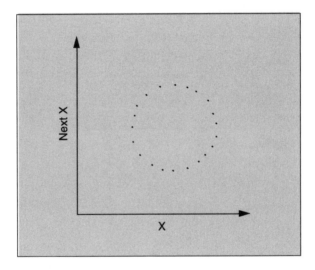

Figure 3-9. Periodic attractor.

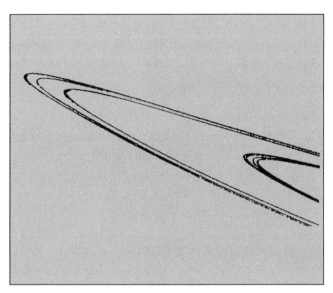

Figure 3-10. Strange attractor.

The system evolves as the values of the current state become the initial values of the next state. Before each loop into the next state, we plot the current system's state in state space.

Modeling systems are easily described with object-oriented techniques for several reasons:

- They can be abstracted easily.

- Every model is related to other models; they share low-level graphics primitives like points and are plotted in space, but they differ in how they generate states.

- Graphics programming in general lends itself to object-oriented techniques.

- A model like object-oriented programming connects the real world to the programming world.

Each type (model) consists of its own characteristics, operations, and constructors. It uses constructors to initialize variables, types to divide the screen into multiple graphic displays, and inheritance to derive related types. Each type explores the world of the strange attractor (nonlinear, chaos, or complexity theory) using the

89

Borland Graphic Interface, included with Turbo C++ and Turbo Pascal, for display. However, if you're using another version of C++ or another graphics toolbox, you can use your own graphics type and still use the general model to send a message with the appropriate coordinate information.

Chaos (or complexity) theory is already changing the way scientists think about the evolution of dynamic systems. Because it's an excellent example of how computers have changed the way we think about the world, we'll look into its background to help you understand all the fuss about chaos and to illustrate an approach for finding types.

Chaos Theory and Strange Attractors

A dynamic system (don't confuse modeling and programming here) is anything you can describe by knowing the value of a variable whose current state depends on its previous states. The state of the system can be something you measure on a continuous scale or something with logical changes. (Is it on? Has something happened since we last checked?)

In a speech-recognition system, for example, each word in a sentence not only carries some individual weight but affects (and is affected by) all the other words in the sentence. Consider the sentence a dynamic system that changes state through the addition of words and punctuation marks. Initially you have nothing (an empty or "no-sentence" state). You add a word and it becomes the new sentence; add a word and the two words are the new sentence; add a word and the three words are the new sentence; add a punctuation mark and the three words plus punctuation are the new sentence; and so on.

When you speak, words necessarily follow each other. When you write, they follow or displace one another. Each new state represents your attempt to clarify the state of the sentence. (But each new state can either clarify or confuse, one reason parsing sentences is so difficult.) The sentence in its next state is very sensitive to its current and previous states.

You could say that meanings are the attractors in the dynamic system. At any state, the sentence may have no meaning (an extinction state), one meaning (a stable state), or many meanings (possibly a chaotic state), depending on any number of things — point of view, reading or writing skill, and so on.

Mathematic Attraction

Folks from many diverse fields are trying to understand dynamic systems. Their discoveries have led to at least one conclusion — anything whose state can change is incredibly complex.

Mathematicians and computer scientists try to wring meaning out of complex systems by representing them with equations and pictures. Some particularly useful pictures exist in state space, where each point holds all the information needed to describe a dynamic system at one time.

For example, suppose a system changes state depending on a variable, such as size or number. Call the variable X and its rate of change R. Then equations like $Nextx = R * X(* (1-X))$ can describe the system.

In this case, 1 represents unity (the entire system or all we can have of it) and 0 represents nothing. Either extreme state (when $Nextx = 1$ or 0) translates into oblivion when $Nextx = 1$ and $Nextx$ is everything.

The previous equation, the so-called standard map or logistic equation, has been studied by mathematically inclined folks in many fields. They've discovered that it (and presumably the dynamic system it describes) behaves unpredictably. In general, any system you describe with a nonlinear equation or equations will behave unpredictably because it's extremely sensitive to initial conditions. Nearby values of X in one state may lead to values of $Nextx$ that are far apart in the next state.

You can complicate matters even further by increasing the number of variables in a system (that is, your representation of a system). For example, two rules for changes in state — $Nextx = AX - (1-(Y*Y))$ and $Nexty = BY$ — can present an infinite number of states (*Nextx* values) responding to infinitely small changes in the condition of the previous state (or *X* value). This infinity of values is the chaotic set for this dynamic system.

You can see this chaos by plotting the values of each state (*Nextx*) in time. The X axis is time; the Y axis is the value of each *X* (Figure 3-11).

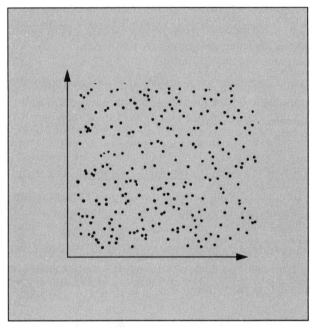

Figure 3-11. Chaos.

There's a certain order in most chaotic systems. One way to see this order is in state space. When we plot values of *Nextx* against values of current *X*, we uncover the attractor for the chaotic set. This attractor lives in state space and consists of all the points in the chaotic set. By mutual agreement, it's called *strange*. Figure 3-12 shows the strange attractor corresponding to the chaotic set in Figure 3-11.

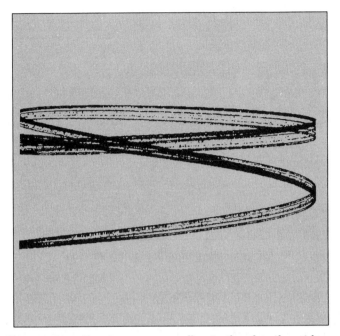

Figure 3-12. The strange attractor corresponding to the chaotic set in Figure 3-11.

The fractal (or self-similar) nature of the system becomes apparent when you zoom in on any area of the attractor. The deeper you go, the more complex (and detailed) the attractor becomes, yet the more orderly it seems.

Inheriting Strange Attractors

Inheritance can help describe and implement a modeling system to create and display strange attractors. Figure 3-13 shows one hierarchy for generating and displaying a model.

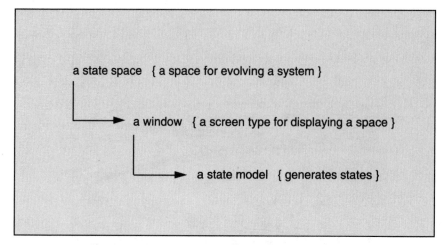

Figure 3-13. A hierarchy for generating and displaying a model.

Any state model will share the characteristics of having a window (a way to display evolving states) and a state space for creating state values without concern for how the space will be displayed. If you decide to reroute the generated states to something other than a window, you can easily change or bypass the window. And since the state space is independent of the display itself, you can display the space anywhere on the screen.

Display Window

A display window is characterized by four variables representing its corners and an initial point in the window. The *Window* constructor initializes the window, draws a border around it, and initializes a point within the window.

You can describe a window like this in C++:

```
class Window {
protected:
  int X,Y;                  // point in window
  int X1, X2, Y1, Y2;       // window location
public:
  Window(int InitX,     int InitY,
         int InitWinX1, int InitWinX2,
```

```
         int InitWinY1, int InitWinY2);
  ~Window() {};
};
```

and like this in Turbo Pascal:

```
WindowPtr = ^Window;
Window = object
  X, Y,                            { point in window }
  X1, X2, Y1, Y2 : integer;        { window location }
  constructor init(InitX,InitY,
                 InitWinX1, InitWinX2,
                 InitWinY1, InitWinY2 : integer);
  destructor Done; virtual;
end;
```

The display window is independent of any model and thus can be treated as a separate object type. Any model will generate values independently of the display-window specifics. These values can then be scaled into a display window.

Three likely candidates for becoming object types are the display window, the state space, and the model generator. Each model will have a state space, where values are initially produced, and a window for displaying the scaled values.

Since a model will need to have both a display window and a state space, we can compose a model out of the object types (display window and state space) or derive a model from them.

If you're a purist, you might object to deriving a model from these components; a model isn't exactly a kind of state space, nor is a state space a kind of display window.

A composed model might look like this in C++:

```
class Model1 {
  float A,B;
public:
  Window DWindow;          // composed
  SSpace StateSpace;
```

```
  Model1(int InitWinX1, int InitWinX2,
         int InitWinY1, int InitWinY2);
  ~Model1(){};
  virtual void Generator();
};
```

and like this in Turbo Pascal:

```
ModelPtr1 = ^Model1;
Model1 = object
  A, B : real;                    { variables in the model }
  DWindow: Window;                { composed of objects }
  SSpace : StateSpace;
  constructor Init;               { Initialize the model. }
  destructor Done; virtual;
  procedure Generator; virtual;   { Generate the model. }
end;
```

One problem with this approach is that it requires you to create and manipulate three objects instead of one. A single object knows about itself, so you don't have to send messages to individual objects. Sometimes more objects are better, of course. In the remainder of this attractor example, I'll opt for nonpurism and derive a model from a state space and display window.

State Space

A state space is an area characterized by four range variables representing its corners and the "zoom factor" of the space. It's derived from a display window. The state-space constructor initializes the space and an initial point in the space and calls the display window to construct itself.

You can describe a state space as follows in C++:

```
class StateSpace : public Window {
protected:
  float Xpoint, Ypoint;
  float SpaceX1;              // boundaries of space
  float SpaceX2;
  float SpaceY1;
```

```
    float SpaceY2;
public:
    StateSpace(int InitX, int InitY,
              int InitWinX1, int InitWinX2,
              int InitWinY1, int InitWinY2,
              float InitXpoint, float InitYpoint,
              float Minx, float Maxx,
              float Miny, float Maxy);
    void Scale();            // Scale space to window.
    ~StateSpace(){};
};
```

and like this in Turbo Pascal:

```
StateSpacePtr = ^StateSpace;
StateSpace = object(Window)
    Xpoint, Ypoint,               { point in space }
    SpaceX1, SpaceX2,
    SpaceY1, SpaceY2 : real;      { boundaries of space }
    constructor Init(InitX, InitY,
                    InitWinX1, InitWinX2,
                    InitWinY1, InitWinY2 : integer;
                    InitXpoint, InitYpoint,
                    Minx, Maxx, Miny, Maxy : real);
    procedure Scale;              { Scale space to window. }
    destructor Done; virtual;
end;
```

Note that the space is independent of the display type; it's the state space of the system without any specific display characteristics.

To display the space on a screen, we send a message to a display window.

Model = State Generator

A state generator creates states for the system. Its constructor also initializes its own variables and sends a message to *Window* to construct itself. In turn, *Window* sends the message to *StateSpace*. The generator (*Model1*) doesn't concern itself with any of *Window*'s or *StateSpace*'s implementation details; it only wants to know that a display window is open and a state space exists.

A state generator (or model) might look like this in C++:

```
class Model1 : public StateSpace {
  float A,B;
public:
  Model1(int InitWinX1, int InitWinX2,
         int InitWinY1, int InitWinY2);
  ~Model1(){};
  virtual void Generator();
};
```

or like this in Turbo Pascal:

```
ModelPtr1 = ^Model1;
Model1 = object (StateSpace)
  A, B : real;                 { variables in the model }
  constructor Init;            { Initialize the model. }
  destructor Done; virtual;
  procedure Generator; virtual;  { Generate the model. }
end;
```

This model generates the Henon attractor, introduced in 1976. Its implementation in C++ is:

```
void Model1::Generator() {
  float TempX, TempY;
  setviewport (X1, Y1, X2, Y2, CLIP_ON);
  TempX = Xpoint;          // Save last state.
  TempY = Ypoint;          // Save last state.
  Xpoint = TempY + 1 - (A * TempX * TempX);    // this model
  Ypoint = B * TempX;                          // this model
  Scale();                 // Scale new state to a window.
  putpixel(X,Y,7);
};
```

This model generates the wild attractor, introduced in 1989. Its implementation in Turbo Pascal is:

```
ModelPtr2 = ^Model2;
Model2 = object (Window)
```

```
  R : real;
  constructor init(InitX, InitY, Minx, Maxx, Miny, Maxy : integer;
                   InitXpoint, InitYpoint,
                   InitRangeX1, InitRangeX2,
                   InitRangeY1, InitRangeY2,
                   Rate : real); { factor for this model }
  destructor Done; virtual;
  procedure Generator; virtual;
end;
```

Since each model has its own space and display, you can display more than one model on the screen (as in Listings 3-1 and 3-2) simultaneously, or even overlap displays.

Where OOP Works Best

People often wonder where object-oriented programming should be used. "Everywhere" is only a slight exaggeration since object-oriented programming is a general-purpose approach to programming. Much like structured programming before it, there are few places where object-oriented programming is not useful.

The best applications for object-oriented programming are those that are likely to require ongoing change and are inherently complex. In fact, the more these two characteristics are true, the greater the benefit of object-oriented programming. Large, complex applications require techniques such as encapsulation and inheritance to make them manageable.

The areas where object-oriented programming are not suitable are quick and dirty programs, where it's probably not worth creating reusable objects (though you might benefit tremendously if you have a library of existing objects to build on), and low-level routines that are time-critical, such as device drivers. Otherwise, if you're developing systems or applications, you'll probably benefit from object-oriented programming. And the more you use it to build reusable objects, the greater the advantage on future projects.

Extending Systems

Object-oriented programming makes it easy to extend systems like these; just add features or reimplement existing ones to create new functions. As programs become larger, they become difficult to understand, maintain, and extend. The use of types can improve understanding and help make programs easier to maintain and extend by reducing the amount of code you need to rewrite.

Object-oriented techniques can reduce confusion, improve programming efficiency, and change the way you think about the relationships between the world and your programs. Sounds pretty good, right? So enjoy what you've learned so far and extend yourself a little more: Stand up and stretch those weary muscles before moving on to the next chapter.

Listing 3-1. Complete C++ attractor.

```
// program AttractP;

#include <graphics.h>
#include <conio.h>
#include <math.h>
#define CLIP_ON 1

class BGI {
public:                         // could be a struct or class.
  int graphdriver;
  int graphmode;
  int errorcode;
};

class Window {
protected:
  int X,Y;                              // point in window
  int X1, X2, Y1, Y2;                   // window location
public:
  Window(int InitX, int InitY,
        int InitWinX1, int InitWinX2,
        int InitWinY1, int InitWinY2);
  ~Window() {};
};
```

```
class StateSpace : public Window {
protected:
  float Xpoint, Ypoint;
  float SpaceX1;                        // boundaries of space
  float SpaceX2;
  float SpaceY1;
  float SpaceY2;
public:
  StateSpace(int InitX, int InitY,
             int InitWinX1, int InitWinX2,
             int InitWinY1, int InitWinY2,
             float InitXpoint, float InitYpoint,
             float Minx, float Maxx, float Miny, float Maxy);
  void Scale();                         // scale space to window
  ~StateSpace(){};
};

class Model1 : public StateSpace {
  float A,B;
public:
  Model1(int InitWinX1, int InitWinX2,
         int InitWinY1, int InitWinY2);
  ~Model1(){};
  virtual void Generator();
};

class Model2 : public StateSpace {
  float R;
public:
  Model2(int InitWinX1, int InitWinX2,
         int InitWinY1, int InitWinY2);
  ~Model2(){};
  virtual void Generator();
};

Window::Window (int InitX, int InitY,
               int InitWinX1, int InitWinX2,
               int InitWinY1, int InitWinY2)
{
  X = InitX;                            // initial point in window
  Y = InitY; X1 = InitWinX1;            // window location
  X2 = InitWinX2;
```

```
   Y1 = InitWinY1;
   Y2 = InitWinY2;
   rectangle (X1, Y1, X2, Y2);
};

StateSpace::StateSpace(int InitX, int InitY,
                    int InitWinX1, int InitWinX2,
                    int InitWinY1, int InitWinY2,
                    float InitXpoint, float InitYpoint,
                    float Minx, float Maxx,
                    float Miny, float Maxy) :
                    Window(InitX,InitY,
                        InitWinX1, InitWinX2,
                        InitWinY1, InitWinY2) {
   SpaceX1 = Minx; SpaceX2 = Maxx;
   SpaceY1 = Miny; SpaceY2 = Maxy;
   Xpoint = InitXpoint; Ypoint = InitYpoint;
};

void StateSpace::Scale() { // Scale point in space to window.

   X = ceil((Xpoint - SpaceX1)/(SpaceX2 - SpaceX1) * (X2 - X1));
   Y =  Y2 - (ceil((Ypoint - SpaceY1)/(SpaceY2 - SpaceY1) *
           (Y2 - Y1)));
};

Model1::Model1(int InitWinX1, int InitWinX2,
            int InitWinY1, int InitWinY2) :
                        StateSpace(0,0,
                        InitWinX1,InitWinX2,
                        InitWinY1,InitWinY2,
                        0.4,0, -1.03, 1.27, -0.3, 0.45) {

// Set factors.
   A = 1.4;
   B = 0.3;
};
```

```
Model2::Model2(int InitWinX1, int InitWinX2,
               int InitWinY1, int InitWinY2) :
                         StateSpace(0,1,
                         InitWinX1,InitWinX2,
                         InitWinY1,InitWinY2,
                         0.4,0, -0.5, 1.0, -1, 0.5) {

// Set factors.
R = 4.0;
};

void Model1::Generator() {
  float TempX, TempY;
  setviewport (X1, Y1, X2, Y2, CLIP_ON);
  TempX = Xpoint;                    // Save last state.
  TempY = Ypoint;                    // Save last state.
  Xpoint = TempY + 1 - (A * TempX * TempX);   // this model
  Ypoint = B * TempX;                          // this model
  Scale();                           // Scale new state to a window.
  putpixel(X,Y,7);
};

void Model2::Generator() {
  float Tempx, Tempy;
  setviewport (X1, Y1, X2, Y2, CLIP_ON);
  Tempx = Xpoint;                    // Save last state.
  Tempy = Ypoint;                    // Save last state.
  Ypoint = Tempx - (1 - (Tempy * Tempy));     // this model
  Xpoint = R * Tempx * (1 - Tempx);            // this model
  Scale();                           // Scale point to a window.
  putpixel(X,Y,7);
};

main()
{
// { BGI stuff }

BGI Graph;
```

```
   Graph.graphdriver = DETECT, Graph.graphmode;
                 // Let the BGI determine what board
                 // you're using.
    initgraph(&Graph.graphdriver, &Graph.graphmode,'');

// Set screen and window dimensions.

   int WX1 = 0;
   int WX2 = ceil(getmaxx()/2 - 5);
   int WY1 = 0;
   int WY2 = ceil(getmaxy()/2 + 150);

// Create a model.

Model1 *M1 =  new Model1(WX1,WX2,WY1,WY2);

// Set screen and window dimensions.

   int WWX1 = ceil(getmaxx()/2 + 5);
   int WWX2 = getmaxx();

// Create a model.

Model2 *M2 =  new Model2(WWX1,WWX2,WY1,WY2);

char cmd;

   for (;;)
     {                             // { Iterate the models. }
     M1->Generator();
     M2->Generator();
    }
   while (cmd = getch() != 'q');
   closegraph();
   delete M1;
   delete M2;
   return 0;
}
```

Listing 3-2. Complete Turbo Pascal attractor.

```
program AttractP;

uses crt, graph;

type

BGI = object
  GraphDriver : Integer;
  GraphMode : Integer;
  ErrorCode : Integer;
end;

WindowPtr = ^Window;
Window = object
  X, Y,                          { point in window }
  X1, X2, Y1, Y2 : integer;      { window location }
  constructor init(InitX,InitY,
                   InitWinX1, InitWinX2,
                   InitWinY1, InitWinY2 : integer);
  destructor Done; virtual;
end;

StateSpacePtr = ^StateSpace;
StateSpace = object(Window)
  Xpoint, Ypoint,                { point in space }
  SpaceX1, SpaceX2,
  SpaceY1, SpaceY2 : real;       { boundaries of space }
  constructor Init(InitX, InitY,
                   InitWinX1, InitWinX2,
                   InitWinY1, InitWinY2 : integer;
                   InitXpoint, InitYpoint,
                   Minx, Maxx, Miny, Maxy : real);
  procedure Scale;               { scale space to window }
  destructor Done; virtual;
end;
```

```
ModelPtr1 = ^Model1;
Model1 = object (StateSpace)
  A, B : real;                    { variables in the model }
  constructor Init;               { initialize the model }
  destructor Done; virtual;
  procedure Generator; virtual;   { generate the model }
end;

ModelPtr2 = ^Model2;
Model2 = object (StateSpace)
  R : real;                       { variable in the model  }
  constructor Init;               { Initialize the model. }
  destructor Done; virtual;
  procedure Generator; virtual;   { Generate the model. }
end;

var
  M1      : ModelPtr1;
  M2      : ModelPtr2;
  Graphic : BGI;

constructor Window.Init (InitX, InitY,
                    InitWinX1, InitWinX2,
                    InitWinY1, InitWinY2 : integer);
begin
  X := InitX;                     { initial point in window }
  Y := InitY;
  X1 := InitWinX1;                { window location }
  X2 := InitWinX2;
  Y1 := InitWinY1;
  Y2 := InitWinY2;
  Rectangle (X1, Y1, X2, Y2);
end;

destructor Window.Done;
begin end;                        { abstract }

constructor StateSpace.Init(InitX, InitY,
                    InitWinX1, InitWinX2,
                    InitWinY1, InitWinY2 : integer;
                    InitXpoint, InitYpoint,
                    Minx, Maxx, Miny, Maxy : real);
```

```
begin
  Xpoint := InitXpoint;
  Ypoint := InitYpoint;              { initial point in a space }
  SpaceX1 := Minx;
  SpaceX2 := Maxx;
  SpaceY1 := Miny;
  SpaceY2 := Maxy;
  Window.Init(InitX,InitY,
              InitWinX1, InitWinX2,
              InitWinY1, InitWinY2);
end;

destructor StateSpace.Done;
begin end;

procedure StateSpace.Scale;
begin                       { Scale point in space to window. }
  If (Xpoint = SpaceX1) then      { a little troubleshooting }
    X := X1;
  If (Xpoint = SpaceX2) then
    X := X2;                          { and here }
  If (Xpoint > SpaceX1) then
    X := round((Xpoint - SpaceX1)/(SpaceX2 - SpaceX1) *
      (X2 - X1));
    Y := Y2 - (round((Ypoint - SpaceY1)/(SpaceY2 - SpaceY1) *
      (Y2 - Y1)));
end;

constructor Model1.Init;
var
   LowX, HighX, LowY, HighY : integer;

begin
  { Set screen and window dimensions. }
  LowX  := 0;
  HighX := round(GetMaxx/2 - 5);
  LowY  := 0;
  HighY := round(GetMaxy/2 + 150);

  { factors }
  A := 1.4;
  B := 0.3;
```

```
   StateSpace.Init(0, 0,              { initial X and Y values }
                   LowX, HighX,
                   LowY, HighY,    { screen/window dimensions }
                   0.4, 0,            { Set InitX and Y points. }
                   -1.03, 1.27, -0.3, 0.45);   { Set scales. }
end;

destructor Model1.Done;
begin end;                             { abstract }

constructor Model2.Init;
var
  LowX,HighX,LowY,HighY : integer;
begin

  { Set screen and window dimensions. }
  LowX  := round(GetMaxx/2 + 5);
  HighX := GetMaxx;
  LowY  := 0;
  HighY := round(GetMaxy/2 + 150);
  R     := 4.0;

  StateSpace.Init(0,1,
                  LowX, HighX,
                  LowY, HighY,
                  0.4, 0, -0.5,
                  1.0, -1, 0.5);
end;


destructor Model2.Done;
begin end;                             { abstract }

procedure Model1.Generator;
var
  TempX, TempY : real;
begin
  SetViewPort (X1, Y1, X2, Y2, True);
  TempX := Xpoint;                { Save last state. }
  TempY := Ypoint;                { Save last state. }
  Xpoint := TempY + 1 - (A * TempX * TempX);   { this model }
  Ypoint := B * TempX;                          { this model }
```

```
    StateSpace.Scale;                { Scale new state to a window. }
    putpixel(X,Y,7);
end;


procedure Model2.generator;
var
    Tempx, Tempy : real;
begin
    SetViewPort (X1, Y1, X2, Y2, True);
    Tempx := Xpoint;                 { Save last state. }
    Tempy := Ypoint;                 { Save last state. }
    Ypoint := Tempx - (1 - (Tempy * Tempy));    { this model }
    Xpoint := R * Tempx * (1 - Tempx);          { this model }
    StateSpace.Scale;                { Scale point to a window. }
    putpixel(X,Y,7);
end;


{————————————————————————}
{ Main program: }
{————————————————————————}


{ main }

begin
    Graph.GraphDriver := Detect;     { Let the BGI determine what }
                                     { board you're using. }
    DetectGraph(Graph.GraphDriver, Graph.GraphMode);
    InitGraph(Graph.GraphDriver, Graph.GraphMode,'');
    if GraphResult <> GrOK then
        begin
            WriteLn('>>Halted on graphics error:',
                    GraphErrorMsg(Graph.GraphDriver));
            Halt(1)
        end;

    { Construct and initialize models. }

    new(M1,Init);
    new(M2,Init);
```

```
   repeat
   begin                    { Iterate the models. }
     M1^.Generator;
     M2^.Generator;
   end;
   until keypressed;
   dispose(M1,done);
   dispose(M2,done);
   CloseGraph;
   RestoreCRTMode;          { back to text }
end.
```

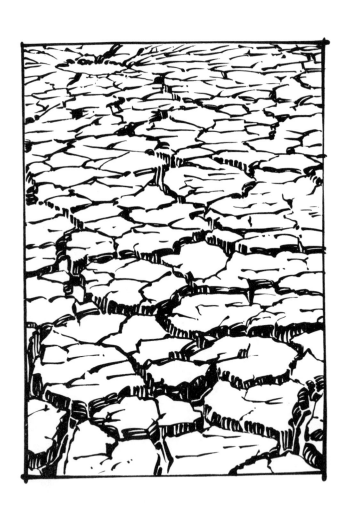

CHAPTER 4

Shaping the System

The Tao is like a well: used but never used up. It's like the eternal void: filled with infinite possibilities. It's hidden but always present.
— Lao-tzu

Since motion and change are essential properties of things, the forces causing the motion are not outside the objects, but are an intrinsic property of matter.
— Fritjof Capra

The word *polymorphism* comes from the Greek meaning "having many shapes." In object-oriented programming, you can create a type and derive new types from it using inheritance. The new derived types inherit characteristics and behaviors from their ancestors. They can also reimplement behaviors and thus change the specific behavior of a type without changing its general interface. This is polymorphism.

Programs you design using polymorphism are easy to maintain, amend, and extend because change doesn't disrupt the system. The messages you send are general; an instance's response to a message is specific.

For example, say you've created a base type in C++. You can derive new types from an existing base type (using inheritance) and allow derived types to reimplement the base type's behavior by making behaviors virtual. In C++:

```
class base {
  int state1;        // private by default
public:                // Make the virtual method accessible.
  virtual void SayWho();
};
```

In Turbo Pascal:

```
base = object
  procedure SayWho; virtual;     { By default, this will be }
                                 { accessible. }
private:                         { Restrict access to current }
  State1 : integer;              { unit. }
end;
```

Since *SayWho* is a virtual method, any type derived from *base* can reimplement *SayWho* however it likes. Using virtual behaviors, you create systems that can send general messages to any variables in a group of types. The system just sends the message; it doesn't need to know how a type will carry it out.

For example, suppose you derive two new types from a base type. In C++:

```
class derived1 : public base {
public:                    // Make this accessible.
  void SayWho();
};

class derived2 : public base {
public:                    // Make this accessible.
  void SayWho();
};
```

In Turbo Pascal:

```
derived1 = object (base)
  procedure SayWho; virtual;     { accessible by default }
end;

derived2 = object (base)
  procedure SayWho; virtual;     { accessible by default }
end;
```

Suppose you then implement *derived1* and *derived2*. In C++:

```
void derived1::SayWho() {       // derived1's behavior
cout << "I'm derived 1";
};
```

```
void derived2::SayWho() {          // derived2's behavior
cout << "I'm derived 2";
};
```

Note the use of *cout*. This predefined stream object for standard output is convenient because it simplifies output formatting. *Cout* can be used to output both built-in and user-defined object types while avoiding the complications of *printf*.

In Turbo Pascal:

```
procedure derived1.SayWho;         { derived1's implementation }
begin
  write('I'm derived 1');
end;

procedure derived2.SayWho;         { derived2's implementation }
begin
  write('I'm derived 2');
end;
```

Now you can send the *SayWho* message to both *derived1* and *derived2*, and each will respond to the message according to its implementation of *SayWho*.

The following piece of cereal code (not to be confused with serial code) illustrates polymorphism in a mouthful. For maximum enjoyment, use a debugger to trace through it. In C++:

```
// CRISPIES.CPP: virtual functions made simple
#include <stdio.h>
struct rice {          // base class
  virtual void talk() {}   // common interface to all types of rice
                 // in-line implementation
                 // different implementations for each type
};

struct snap : rice {
  void talk() { puts("SNAP!"); }          // in-line implementation
};
```

```
struct crackle : rice {
  void talk() { puts("CRACKLE!"); }      // in-line
};

struct pop : rice {
  void talk() { puts("POP!"); }          // in-line
};

main() {
  rice * bowl[] = { new snap, new crackle, new pop };
                    // C++ aggregate initialization
  for(int i = 0; i < sizeof(bowl)/sizeof(bowl[0]); i++)
  bowl[i]->talk();  // Send one talk message to bowl.
}
```

In Turbo Pascal, you can do something similar:

```
type
RicePtr = ^Rice;
Rice = object                { base class }
  constructor Init;
  procedure talk; virtual; { common interface to all types of }
                           { rice }
end;

SnapPtr = ^Snap;
Snap = object(rice)
  constructor Init;
  procedure talk; virtual; { "SNAP" }
end;

CracklePtr = ^Crackle;
Crackle = object(rice)
  constructor Init;
  procedure talk; virtual; { "CRACKLE!" }
end;

PopPtr = ^Pop;
Pop = object(rice)
  constructor Init;
  procedure talk; virtual; { "POP!" }
end;
```

```
{ constructors }
constructor Rice.Init;      { There's no in-line feature in }
begin                       { Turbo Pascal. }
end;

{ methods }
procedure Rice.talk;        { common interface to all types }
begin                       { of rice }
end;

procedure Snap.talk;        { specific Snap behavior }
begin
  writeln('Snap!');
end;

procedure Crackle.talk;     { specific Crackle behavior }
begin
  writeln('Crackle!');
end;

procedure Pop.talk;         { specific Pop behavior }
begin
  writeln('Pop!');
end;

{ main }
var
  Bowl : RicePtr;           { New requires a pointer to a type }
                            { as its first parameter. }
begin
  Bowl := New(SnapPtr,Init);{ Allocate memory and construct. }
    Bowl^.talk;             { Talk message produces a Snap. }
  Bowl := New(CracklePtr,Init);
    Bowl^.talk;             { Talk message produces a Crackle. }
  Bowl := New(PopPtr,Init);
    Bowl^.talk;             { Talk message produces a Pop. }
end.
```

The virtual function *talk* establishes an interface to the various derived types of rice — *Snap*, *Crackle*, and *Pop*. (*Rice* is abstract and thus only exists as an interface to the derived types.) Thus, you can send one message, *talk*, and the correct behavior results.

Note that Turbo Pascal's *New* procedure requires a pointer as the first parameter, while C++ requires a type (in this case, an object type). More on that later.

Figure 4-1 is a different kind of illustration. The *talk* message sent to *Rice* will produce specific *Snap*, *Crackle*, and *Pop* behavior.

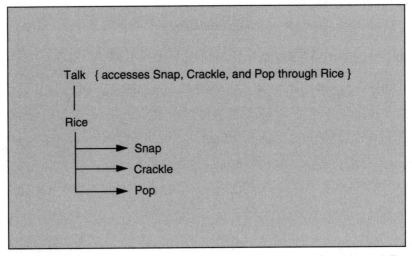

Figure 4-1. The *talk* message sent to *Rice* will produce *Snap, Crackle*, and *Pop* behavior.

Dynamics

Using polymorphism, you can take generalization a step further and send messages to any number of types (derived from a base type) without knowing how the types will behave or even what the types are. You need to:

- Define a base type with virtual methods (a common interface)
- Use inheritance to derive new types
- Create a container/collection to hold dynamically created instances
- Implement a method for accessing the list.

Since you're going to create dynamic types whose sizes aren't necessarily known at compile time, let's backtrack for a moment and discuss how a compiler allocates memory for instances of types.

When you create an instance of a type at compile time by declaring a local variable, the compiler allocates memory for the variable on the stack at compile time. You can do that in C++ with *int Number* and in Turbo Pascal with *Number : integer*.

You can create an instance of a type at run time (on the Turbo Pascal heap or in the C++ free-memory store) by using a pointer containing the address of a variable. In C++, you can declare a pointer to a built-in type with *int* Number*. In Turbo Pascal, it's *NumberPtr : ^integer*.

In object-oriented programming, you can declare an instance of a user-defined type at run time (dynamically) and simultaneously initialize it. This would be complicated if you had to do all the work; fortunately, C++ and Turbo Pascal do most of it for you through the built-in operators *new* and *delete* (in C++), the procedures *New* and *Dispose* (in Turbo Pascal), and constructors and destructors.

For example, you can create and initialize an instance of *SomeCoordinates* in one step. In C++, you declare a pointer to the type and assign the result of the expression *new type* to the pointer:

```
AnyCoordinates * SomeCoordinates = new AnyCoordinates(1,1);
```

SomeCoordinates, a pointer to the type *AnyCoordinates*, gets the address of a block of memory large enough to hold an instance of *AnyCoordinates*. An *AnyCoordinates* constructor is then called automatically to initialize an instance of *AnyCoordinates* with the values 1,1.

In Turbo Pascal, you call *New* with two parameters, a pointer to the type and a constructor that specifies how a new object type will be created:

```
var
  SomeCoordinates : AnyCoordinates;
  Co_Ptr : ^SomeCoordinates;
  New(AnyCoordinates(Co_Ptr, Init(1,1));
```

Memory deallocation is handled in C++ by *delete* and in Turbo Pascal by *Dispose* and a destructor. In C++, the *delete* operator is used to destroy an instance of a type:

```
delete Pointer_to_type;
```

Any destructor you've defined for the type is automatically called when *delete* executes.

In Turbo Pascal, the procedure *Dispose* has been extended to take a second parameter, a destructor:

```
var
  N : TypePtr;
  Dispose(N,Done);
```

Done is the destructor for this type and must be specified explicitly. (Unlike C++, Turbo Pascal doesn't automatically call constructors and destructors for you.) During this call, *Done* looks up the size of the instance in the type's Virtual Method Table (VMT) and passes the size to *Dispose. Dispose* deallocates the memory used by the instance.

Note: Each user-defined object type in Turbo Pascal that has or inherits virtual methods or has a constructor has a VMT associated with it. The compiler automatically creates the VMT through the type's constructor. (The C++ equivalent of the VMT, the VTABLE, isn't created through the constructor; the value of the VPTR is initialized in the constructor.) If a type has virtual methods, you must send a message to the object type's instance constructor before you send the first message to a method. Otherwise, if range checking is off, the compiler leaps into the ozone. It's a good idea to turn on range checking when testing code.

Constructors, Destructors, and Responsibility

Constructors and destructors are used to both initialize field values and, more importantly, allocate and deallocate memory for dynamic objects. You should always write your constructors and destructors so that they take full responsibility for creating and destroying dynamic objects. This means that if some action must have occurred before a kind of object is used (read a data file, reset some device, and so on), it should take place in the constructor that initializes the object. No other steps should be required to use an object since the object itself should be responsible for these things. It also means that the construction process should in turn allocate memory for any other objects it contains.

When deallocating an object, you should deallocate any memory it uses without disposing of any objects allocated in the constructor. For example, when disposing of a linked list, you must also dispose of each node it contains. An easy way to do that is to call the destructor of each node object. That way, if the nodes themselves allocate other objects, they'll dispose of those objects in their destructor. The general rule is that objects should allocate and deallocate the things for which they are responsible.

Managing From the Bottom Up

A linked list is an excellent data structure for problems involving data elements whose exact size, shape, and number aren't known at compile time. In this example, you'll define and implement a type, called a *cell manager*, that manipulates a linked list of cells. Those cells are instances of types. A linked list (also a type) consists of cells and the methods needed to manipulate the cells.

Cells consist of a node (a pointer to the next cell) and any type: string, real, integer, or user-defined.

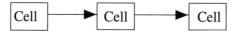

The cell manager can process the list without knowing exactly which type a cell contains. Each cell is an instance of a specific type and links to the next cell through a pointer:

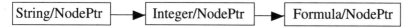

At the heart of the cell manager are three types: a base type that defines the interface to a group of types, a cell, and a linked list to connect cells.

The base type consists of a destructor, which guarantees that every type derived from *Base* will have a destructor as well. (In this example, *Base* serves as a check and could be omitted.)

The base type looks like this in C++:

```
class Base {
public:
  virtual ~Base();
};
```

and like this in Turbo Pascal:

```
Base = object
  destructor Done; virtual;
end;
```

A cell consists of a pointer to the next cell (a link), a constructor (to create the cell), a destructor (to delete it), and a virtual method for handling itself. *Cell* is the interface for a group of cells that will reimplement their own behaviors. Any type derived from *Cell* will automatically have a link (the pointer) to the next cell. In C++:

```
class Cell : public Base {
  Cell *Next;              // a pointer to the next cell
public:
  Cell() {};               // in-line
  ~Cell(){};               // in-line
  virtual void Action(){}; // In-line: each cell will reimple-
};                         // ment Action to suit itself.
```

In Turbo Pascal:

```
CellPtr = ^Cell;
Cell = object
  Next: CellPtr;                   { a pointer to the next cell }
  constructor Init;
  destructor Done; virtual;
  procedure Action; virtual;       { Each cell will reimplement }
end;                               { Action to suit itself. }
```

Note that C++ lets you declare the pointer type within the class itself, while Turbo Pascal's C*ellPtr* declaration precedes that of *Cell*.

Since there's no best way to implement a linked list in both C++ and Turbo Pascal, the following fragments (and the complete source code in Listings 4-1 and 4-2) show two alternatives. You can, for example, create a list by first creating a node consisting of a pointer to a cell (or any type derived from *Cell*), a pointer to the next node (a link), and a constructor and destructor. In C++:

```
struct Node {                    // The list item can be Cell or
  Cell *Item;                    // any class derived from Cell.
  Node  *Next;                   // pointer to next Node type
  Node(Cell *F, Node *N) : Item = F; Next = N; {}
                                 // constructor
  ~Node() { delete Item;}        // destructor
};
```

A cell list might then consist of a pointer to a node, a constructor for creating a node, and methods for managing cells:

```
class CellList {                 // List of types pointed to by
  Node *Nodes;                   // Nodes points to a node.
public:
  CellList(){ Nodes = NULL; }    // constructor
  ~CellList();                   // destructor
  void Add(Cell *NewItem);       // Add a new cell to the list.
  void Manipulate();
};
```

The *Add* method adds a node — an instance of a cell or any type derived from a cell — to the list:

```
void CellList::Add(Cell *NewItem)
{
  Nodes = new Node(NewItem, Nodes);
}
```

Add accepts a pointer to a cell or any type derived from a cell and can add a cell without knowing its specific type.

The *Manipulate* method sends a message to each instance of the object type telling it to act according to its own implementation of the *Action* behavior:

```
void CellList::Manipulate()
{
  Node* Current = Nodes;          // Start at top of list.
  while (Current)                 // Do until end of list.
  {
    Current->Item->Action();      // Evaluate this node.
    Current = Current->Next;      // Point to the next node.
  };
};
```

Like *Add*, *Manipulate* doesn't know how any cell will behave; it just sends them general messages, and each cell takes care of itself (see Figure 4-2).

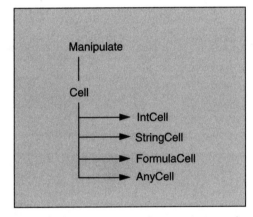

Figure 4-2. *Manipulate* **sends the cells general messages, and each cell takes care of itself.**

Another approach to creating a linked list of cells omits the separate creation of a node. In Turbo Pascal:

```
CellListPtr = ^CellList;
CellList = object(Base)
  Last: CellPtr;                  { end of list }
  constructor Init;
  destructor Done; virtual;
  procedure Add(N: CellPtr);      { Add new cell to list. }
```

```
function Next(N: CellPtr): CellPtr;   { Return a pointer }
                                      { to the next cell. }
procedure Manipulate; virtual;  { Process CellList; }
                                { controls that can manipulate }
                                { any cell regardless of type. }
end;
```

As in the previous C++ example, the method A*dd* adds a new cell to the list:

```
procedure CellList.Add(N: CellPtr);     { Add gets a pointer }
                                        { to a cell. }
begin
  if Last = nil then Last := N
  else N^.Next := Last^.Next;
  Last^.Next := N;
  Last := N;
end;
```

Manipulate processes the list using nodes (instances of cell types) without knowing the specifics of any instance:

```
procedure CellList.Manipulate;   { Process the cell list. }
var
  P : CellPtr;
begin
  P := CellPtr(Last^.Next);        { Set pointer to first node. }
  while P <> nil do
  begin
    P^.Action;                     { generic message to all cells }
    P := CellPtr(Next(P));         { Get pointer to next node. }
  end;
end;
```

Cell is an abstract type; it contains no data. However, you use it to derive specific types: string cell, integer cell, formula cell, and so on. The abstract type defines the general characteristics and behaviors of a group of related subtypes. In a spreadsheet, for example, any cell might contain numerical data (reals or integers), methods for handling data (formulas), names (strings), and so on.

A string cell might look like this in C++:

```
class StringCell : public Cell {
  char *Value;
public:
  StringCell(char *V);
  ~StringCell() {};            // in-line destructor
  void Action();               // Process a StringCell.
};
```

and like this in Turbo Pascal:

```
StringCellPtr = ^StringCell;
StringCell = object(Cell)
  Value: StringPtr;
  constructor Init(V: String);
  destructor Done; virtual;
  procedure Action; virtual;     { Process a StringCell. }
end;
```

The virtual *Action* method will determine how *StringCell* processes itself. An integer cell might look similar. In C++:

```
class IntCell : public Cell {
  int Number;
public:
  IntCell(int V);
  ~IntCell() {};           // in-line destructor
  void Action();           // Process an IntCell.
};
```

In Turbo Pascal:

```
IntCellPtr = ^IntCell;
IntCell = object(Cell)
  Number: integer;
  constructor Init(V: integer);
  destructor Done; virtual;
  procedure Action; virtual;     { Process an IntCell. }
end;
```

A formula cell might look like this in C++:

```
class FormulaCell : public Cell {
  char *Formula;
public:
  FormulaCell(char *V);
  ~FormulaCell() {};        // in-line destructor
  void Action();            // Process a Formula.
};
```

and like this in Turbo Pascal:

```
FormulaCellPtr = ^FormulaCell;
FormulaCell = object(Cell)
  Formula: StringPtr;
  constructor Init(V: String);
  destructor Done; virtual;
  procedure Action; virtual;      { Process a Formula. }
end;
```

Any new cell derived from *Cell* need only declare its own data and reimplement the *Action* method. The general *Manipulation* method inherited from *CellList* controls the action.

To access the entire list of cells, you can send one message — *manipulate* — and let each cell respond to it according to how the object type has implemented the method. Figure 4-3 shows the complete object hierarchy for this example.

Tracing Through Pointers

If you're new to using pointers, it can be helpful to trace through them interactively with a debugger. In Turbo C++ or Turbo Pascal, you can do this by putting breakpoints in your program where you create or use dynamic objects. You can then use the *Debug Evaluate* menu command to enter an expression that refers to some pointer.

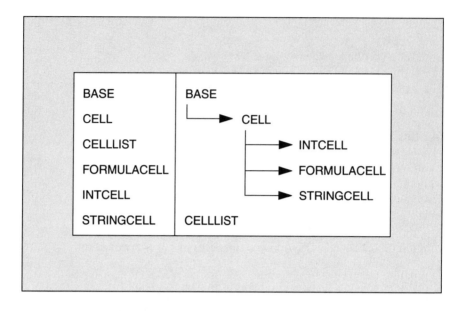

Figure 4-3. The complete object hierarchy.

For example, suppose you were looking at the code for the Pascal method *CellList.Manipulate* shown earlier. This method sets a variable *P* to the first item in the list. If you enter *P* in the expression field and press Return, the debugger will display the address to which it refers. Entering *P^* will display the object *P* points to, which is usually more interesting.

To look at the next pointer in the list, enter *P^.Next*. To see its contents, enter *P^.Next^*. You can continue tracing through the list by evaluating the expressions *P^.Next^.Next^*, *P^.Next^.Next^.Next^*, and so on to examine pointers and their contents until you feel more comfortable with them.

Some Advantages

Object-oriented programming techniques have significantly increased programmers' potential to create more complex programs. It's much easier to get a prototype up and running quickly in C++ or Turbo Pascal than in conventional structured languages, and large programs are easier to extend and maintain.

By considering a program a hierarchy of types and thinking of the general (or abstract) case while solving problems, you can significantly increase your productivity. Inheritance hierarchies are conceptually simple and flexible. Programs designed to use polymorphism and dynamic techniques are powerful and extensible.

In C++ and Turbo Pascal, the ability to create and destroy variables at run time is important enough that it's part of both languages. When you create a user-defined data type, you can easily make a dynamic variable of that type.

This means you can build an object-oriented program that doesn't need to know the number or type of objects involved in a problem before it begins to solve it. This fits beautifully with our world, where we seldom know all the tools we need when we begin working on a project. Object-oriented languages allow us to write programs that adapt to unexpected situations.

Listing 4-1. C++ cell manager.

```
// program cells

#include <string.h>
#include <iostream.h>
#include <stdlib.h>

class Base
{
public:
   ~Base();
};
```

```
class Cell : public Base {
public:
    Cell *Next;                    // a pointer to the next cell
    Cell() {};                     // in-line
    virtual ~Cell(){};             // in-line
    virtual void Action(){};       // Each cell will reimplement its
};                                 // own Action to suit itself.

struct Node {                      // The list item can be Cell or
    Cell *Item;                    // any class derived from Cell.
    Node  *Next;                   // pointer to next Node type
    Node(Cell *F, Node *N) : Item = F; Next = N; {} // constructor
    ~Node() { delete Item;}        // destructor
};

class CellList {                   // List of types pointed to by
    Node *Nodes;                   // Nodes points to a node.
public:
    // constructor
    CellList() : { Nodes = NULL; }
    // destructor
    ~CellList();
    // Add an item to CellList.
    void Add(Cell *NewItem);

    // List the items.
    void Manipulate();
};

class StringCell : public Cell {
public:
    char *Value;
    StringCell(char *V);
    ~StringCell() {};                       // in-line destructor
    void Action();                          // Process a StringCell.
};

class IntCell : public Cell {
public:
    int Number;
    IntCell(int V);
```

```
    ~IntCell() {};                   // in-line destructor
    void Action();                   // Process an IntCell.
};

class FormulaCell : public Cell {
public:
    char *Formula;
    FormulaCell(char *V);
    ~FormulaCell() {};               // in-line destructor
    void Action();                   // Process a Formula.
};

// constructors

StringCell::StringCell(char *V) {
    int length = strlen(V);
    Value = new char[length + 1];
    strcpy(Value,V);
};

IntCell::IntCell(int V) {
    Number = V;
};

FormulaCell::FormulaCell(char *V) {
    int length = strlen(V);
    Formula = new char[length + 1];
    strcpy(Formula,V);
};

// methods

void StringCell :: Action() {
    cout << Value << "\n";           // Just write the string.
};

void IntCell :: Action() {
    cout << Number << "\n";          // Write the integer.
};
```

```
void FormulaCell :: Action() {
    cout << Formula << "\n";        // Just write the formula
};                                  // for now.


// member functions for List class

CellList::~CellList()               // destructor
{
    while (Nodes) {                 // until end of list
      Node *N = Nodes;              // Get node pointed to.
      Nodes = Nodes->Next;          // Point to next node.
      delete N;                     // Delete pointer's memory.
    };
}


void CellList::Add(Cell *NewItem)
{
    Nodes = new Node(NewItem, Nodes);
}


void CellList::Manipulate()
{
    Node *Current = Nodes;
    while (Current)
    {
      Current->Item->Action();      // Evaluate this node.
      Current = Current->Next;      // Point to the next node.
    };
}

// Main program
main()
{
    char CurrentChar = ' ';
    char *S;
    int I;

    CellList AList;
```

```
while (CurrentChar != '~')      // ~ says there are no more
{                               // cells to initialize.
  cout << "Enter cell value: ";      // Add instances of cell
                                // types by evaluating input.

  cin >> S;
  CurrentChar = S[0];           // Determine type from first
                                // char.
  switch (CurrentChar) {
  case '#':
    AList.Add(new FormulaCell(S));  // # indicates a formula.
    break;
  case '1':
  case '2':
  case '3':
  case '4':
  case '5':
  case '6':
  case '7':
  case '8':
  case '9':
  case '0':                        // It's a number.
    I = atoi(S);
    AList.Add(new IntCell(I));
    break;
  default :                        // It's a string.
    AList.Add(new StringCell(S));
  };
};
  AList.Manipulate();
}
```

Listing 4-2. Turbo Pascal cell manager.

```
program cells;
uses CRT, DOS;

type

StringPtr = ^String;
```

```
Base = object
   destructor Done; virtual;
end;

CellPtr = ^Cell;
Cell = object(Base)
   Next: CellPtr;                   { a pointer to the next cell }
   constructor Init;
   destructor done; virtual;
   procedure Action; virtual;       { Each cell will reimplement }
end;                                 { Action to suit itself. }

CellListPtr = ^CellList;
CellList = object
   Last: CellPtr;                   { the end of the list }
   constructor Init;
   destructor Done; virtual;
   procedure Add(N: CellPtr);       { Add a new cell to the list. }
   function Next(N: CellPtr): CellPtr; { Return a pointer to }
                                    { the next cell. }
   procedure Manipulate; virtual;   { Process CellList; }
           { controller that can manipulate any cell }
           { regardless of the type it's an instance of. }
end;

StringCellPtr = ^StringCell;
StringCell = object(Cell)
   Value: StringPtr;
   constructor Init(V: String);
   destructor Done; virtual;
   procedure Action; virtual;              { Process a StringCell. }
end;

IntCellPtr = ^IntCell;
IntCell = object(Cell)
   Number: integer;
   constructor Init(V: integer);
   destructor Done; virtual;
   procedure Action; virtual;              { Process an IntCell. }
end;
```

```
FormulaCellPtr = ^FormulaCell;
FormulaCell = object(Cell)
   Formula: StringPtr;
   constructor Init(V: String);
   destructor Done; virtual;
   procedure Action; virtual;              { Process a Formula. }
end;

{ constructors }

constructor Cell.init;
begin
end;

constructor CellList.Init;
begin
   Last := nil;
end;

constructor StringCell.Init(V: String);
begin
   GetMem(Value, Length(V) + 1);
   Value^ := V;
end;

constructor IntCell.Init(V: integer);
begin
   Number := V;
end;

constructor FormulaCell.Init(V: string);
begin
   GetMem(Formula, Length(V) + 1);
   Formula^ := V;                          { Formula gets V. }
{ In a more complex example, you might parse the formula here. }
end;

{ destructors }

destructor Base.Done;
begin
end;
```

```
destructor Cell.Done;
begin
end;

destructor CellList.Done;
begin
end;

destructor StringCell.Done;
begin
   FreeMem(Value, Length(Value^) + 1);
end;

destructor FormulaCell.Done;
begin
end;

destructor IntCell.Done;
begin
end;

{ methods }

procedure Cell.Action;
begin
end;

procedure StringCell.Action;
begin
   writeln(Value^);                  { Just write the string. }
end;

procedure IntCell.Action;
var
   S : string;
begin
   Str(Number,S);
   writeln(S);                       { Write the integer. }
end;
```

```
procedure FormulaCell.Action;
begin
   writeln(Formula^);              { Just write the formula }
end;                               { for now. }


{ cell list methods }

procedure CellList.Add(N: CellPtr);     { a pointer here, so any }
                                        { type or descendant of type }
                                        { can be passed }
begin
   if Last = nil then Last := N
   else N^.Next := Last^.Next;
   Last^.Next := N;
   Last := N;
end;


function CellList.Next(N: CellPtr): CellPtr;   { Return a pointer }
                                               { to the next cell. }
begin
   if N = Last then Next := nil
   else Next := N^.Next;
end;


procedure CellList.Manipulate;   { Process the cell list. }
var
   P : CellPtr;
begin
   P := CellPtr(Last^.Next);      { Set pointer to first node. }
   while P <> nil do              { until the end of the list }
   begin
     P^.Action;                   { message to each cell }
     P := CellPtr(Next(P));       { Set pointer to next node. }
   end;
end;

procedure InitCells(L : CellListPtr);   { Initialize all cells }
                                        { at once. }
var
   CurrentChar : char;
   S : string;
   I, Code : integer;
```

```
begin
    while CurrentChar <> '~' do    { ~ says there are no more }
                                   { cells to initialize. }
    begin
      writeln('Enter cell value: '); { Add instances of cell }
                                   { types by evaluating input. }
      readln(S);
      CurrentChar := S[1];         { Determine type from first }
      case CurrentChar of          { char. }
      '#' : L^.Add(New(FormulaCellPtr,Init(S)));
                                   { # indicates a formula. }
      '1','2','3','4','5','6','7','8','9','0' :{ It's a number. }
      begin
        Val(S,I,Code);
        L^.Add(New(IntCellPtr,Init(I)));
      end;
      else                         { It's a string. }
        L^.Add(New(StringCellPtr,Init(S)));
      end;                         { case }
    end;
end;

{ main }

var
    Pointer_to_list : CellListPtr;

begin
    Clrscr;
    new(Pointer_to_list,Init);     { Initialize a new cell list on }
                                   { the heap.}
    { Note: new's first parameter must be a pointer. }
    InitCells(Pointer_to_list);
    Pointer_to_list^.Manipulate;   { Process the cell list. }
    Dispose(Pointer_to_list,Done);     { Clean up. }
end. { main }
```

CHAPTER 5

Dynamic Style

Blunt your sharpness, untie your knots, soften your glare,
settle your dust.

— Lao-tzu

The use of polymorphic types is fundamental to object-oriented programming. A type is polymorphic if it uses virtual methods and has a method whose name is shared by more than one type in the hierarchy.

For example, in a hierarchy of musical scales, the method name *Play_minor_scale* can be shared by all musical keys. Each key actually implements its minor scale using different notes, but the message *Play_minor_scale* can be carried out without the sender's knowing the specifics of each key's implementation (see Figure 5-1).

Although you can create an instance of a polymorphic object on the stack without using pointers, creating an instance at run time is convenient and useful. You can do this by allocating it on the heap using a pointer. Both C++ and Turbo Pascal make manipulation of dynamic variables easy and efficient through the *new* and *delete* operators in C++ and the *New* and *Dispose* procedures in Turbo Pascal.

To create an instance of a dynamic variable in C++, you pass *new* the type to be created:

```
new(Shape);
```

In Turbo Pascal, you pass *New* a pointer to the instance of the type to be created:

```
var ShapePointer : ^Shape;
New(ShapePointer);
```

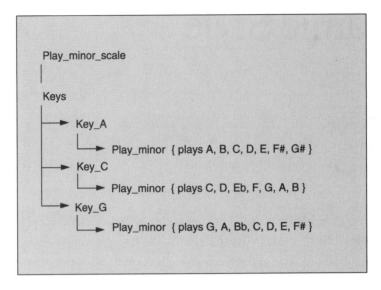

Figure 5-1. The message _Play_minor_scale_ can be carried out without the sender's knowing the specifics of each key's implementation.

As with *struct*s (in C++) and *record*s (in Turbo Pascal), *new* allocates enough space on the heap for an instance of the pointer's base type and returns that space's address via the pointer. If the dynamic variable contains any virtual methods, you must use a constructor to initialize the type before sending any messages to the object. You can allocate space and initialize the instance of the type in one call. In C++:

```
Circle *ThisCircle = new Circle(140, 75, 50 );  // points and radius
```

In Turbo Pascal:

```
var
  CirclePtr : ^Circle;

New(CirclePtr,Init(140,75,50));   { points and radius }
```

Dynamic variables are useful because you can add any number of instances of them at run time without knowing the exact number of instances at compile time.

By delaying system-determining decisions until run time, you disconnect the code from a type's details and the system becomes more flexible. A working system can be modified and adjusted long after it's "finished." And you can add instances of new types to the system without disrupting it.

Returning to our musical example, you can add a new key to the system by deriving it from *Keys* and let each descendant implement the *Play_minor_scale* behavior in its own way. In C++:

```
class Keys {
public:
  Keys(); { }
  ~Keys(); { }
  virtual void Play_minor_scale(); { }  // Will be reimplemented
                                        // by ancestors.
}

class Key_F : public Keys {
public:
  Key_F(); { }
  ~Key_F(); { }
  void Play_minor_scale();   // Implement specific play behavior.
};
```

In Turbo Pascal:

```
Keys = object
  constructor Init;
  destructor Done; virtual;
  procedure Play_minor_scale; virtual;  { Will be reimplemented }
end;                                     { by descendants. }

Key_F = object(Keys)
  constructor Init;
  destructor Done; virtual;
  procedure Play_minor_scale; virtual;
end;
```

The next example shows how to create a frame-based expert system and maintain it in a linked list of polymorphic types. *Frame* is just a synonym (in the artificial intelligence world) for a type consisting of characteristics and behaviors.

Expert Systems

Expert systems lend themselves particularly well to object-oriented programming techniques. These systems let nonexperts do the work of experts, simplify complex operations, and automate repetitive processes.

Through a knowledge base of expert information, they map the input characteristics and behaviors of a system, problem, pattern, or object. Input characteristics and behaviors represent colors, sizes, processes, events, symptoms, and so on. Output represents a solution, advice, pattern match, decision, and so on. Figure 5-2 illustrates this idea.

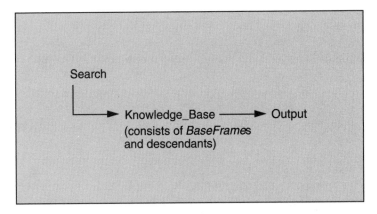

Figure 5-2. Expert systems map the input characteristics and behaviors of a system, problem, pattern, or object.

The information in an expert system's knowledge base is put there by an expert who has skill or knowledge in a specific domain. This information is almost certainly dynamic — needing to be updated, corrected, and so on. A new expert, for example, might contribute new information. The system itself might generate new information or even correct itself. What this means for developers is that an expert system should be built so that it can evolve easily.

An expert system's inference engine can map input characteristics to some output behavior in two ways, usually referred to as *backward chaining* and *forward chaining*.

A backward-chaining model reasons from known results back toward the current state of the world. For example, a set of symptoms might chain back to a disease having those symptoms. The system finds a match by selecting a disease and asking whether the user has the symptoms of that disease. In an *or*-based system (*Symptom1 or Symptom2*), a single symptom usually produces a match. In an *and*-based system (*Symptom1 and Symptom2*), all symptoms must be present to produce a match. The system works from a disease back to the symptoms until it finds a disease that matches.

A forward-chaining system reasons from the current state of the world toward a result or solution. For example, you might inform the system of your symptoms first and ask it to find the correct disease. In this case, the system works from the symptoms to the disease.

In this chapter, we'll construct a forward-chaining model whose knowledge base consists of frames. We'll use all the key elements of object-oriented programming and thus be able to:

- Create instances of object types at run time
- Modify a type's behavior and derive new types without disrupting the working system
- Maintain the hierarchy of types in a linked list
- Modify the mechanisms that manipulate the lists without disrupting the types.

You can, for example, continue to use the list machinery as is and change the knowledge base to hold other types of information. The list handler doesn't need to know which object types it's sending messages to; it just sends messages and the objects handle themselves. Thus, you can let any type determine whether it's the correct one in the knowledge base to produce output for the problem.

OOP in AI

Object-oriented programming is used extensively in artificial intelligence applications ranging from expert systems to pattern-recognition programs, diagnostic programs, learning programs, natural-language parsers, and neural networks. Traditionally, AI work has been done using specialized languages like LISP and Prolog. LISP was developed in the 1950s and is based on the manipulation of lists of symbols. It doesn't make a distinction between code and data, so programs themselves are lists of special symbols that define functions. LISP is considered a flexible language, but it's also primitive; it has few built-in types or functions.

Prolog emerged in the 1980s as the preferred way of doing AI programming in Europe. It's based on the idea of logic programming, where programs query or manipulate a database of facts and rules. This higher-level language is very good at implementing expert systems because it contains a built-in inference engine for resolving complex queries.

Not surprisingly, object-oriented versions of LISP and Prolog have been developed. LISP-based languages that have objects include Loops, Flavors, XLisp, and CLOS. XLisp, one of the most affordable LISP implementations, is freely distributed by its author, David Betz, and is available for almost all computers. Several object-oriented variations of Prolog are available; the most widely used is Prolog++.

Despite their flexibility for AI applications, LISP and Prolog are not widely used outside of research areas. For many programmers, C++ and Turbo Pascal are considered more efficient, though perhaps not as flexible, for AI programming.

Frames vs. Objects

Some AI languages implement a more flexible type of frame that has many of the same characteristics as objects. Think of a frame as consisting of slots that have facets. Frames can be used to derive "fuzzy knowledge" based on rules stored in the frames themselves. For example, you could describe animals through frames that explain some of the default characteristics and provide rules for determining information that's not directly stored.

In this case, we might have a *Marsupial* frame that has slots for what it eats and where it lives. The facets for these slots could specify that the default values are *Eucalyptus* and *In Australia*. We could also have a special slot called *AKO* for "a-kind-of." This could be used to say that a *Kangaroo* is a kind of *Marsupial*. This gives a kind of inheritance between the *Kangaroo* and *Marsupial* frames. In very flexible frame-based systems, the rules for evaluating slots and the relationships between frames can be changed dynamically at run time.

Finding the Objects

Let's begin by envisioning the kinds of types we'll need. When you design a system around types, try to think simply first and extend your ideas later. The more you can think in the abstract, the better.

This expert system will consist of a template of characteristics to evaluate (input characteristics), an inference engine (rules for mapping input to output), a knowledge base of expert information (which the inference engine will use to infer output), and output behaviors (results).

Let's first create an abstract *BaseFrame*, the base type for our expert system. *BaseFrame* will consist of a constructor and a destructor and serve as the ancestor for the frames derived from it. In C++:

```
class BaseFrame {
public:
  BaseFrame(); {}
  virtual ~BaseFrame(); {}
  virtual void input(); {}      // Get input characteristics for
                                // comparison.
  virtual void eval(); {}       // Evaluate input
                                // characteristics.
  virtual void output(); {}     // Determine output behavior.
};
```

In Turbo Pascal:

```
BaseFramePtr : ^BaseFrame;
BaseFrame = object
  constructor Init;
  destructor Done; virtual;
  procedure Input; virtual;        { Get input. }
  procedure Eval; virtual;         { Evaluate input using derived }
                                   { Frame's rule. }
  procedure Output;virtual;        { Determine output. }
end;

constructor BaseFrame.Init;
begin
end;

destructor BaseFrame.Done;
begin
end;

procedure BaseFrame.Input;
begin
end;

procedure BaseFrame.Eval;
begin
end;

procedure BaseFrame.Output;
begin
end;
```

To keep this expert system pertinent, say it contains information about sports teams and the behaviors for getting input and determining correct output. The correct output might correspond to predictions about how well this team is expected to do in its next game.

SportsFrame, then, is an object type containing information about a sports team. In C++:

```
class SportsFrame : public BaseFrame {
public:
  int Total_points;          // this team's characteristics
```

```
    int Points_against;
    int Wins;
    int Losses;
    int Cur_Tp;              // input characteristics to compare with
    int Cur_Pa;              // this team's characteristics
    int Cur_W;
    int Cur_L;

    SportsFrame(int I1, int I2, int I3, int I4)
    // constructor for creating a frame
       { Total_points = I1;   // in-line initialization
         Points_against = I2;
         Wins = I3;
         Losses = I4;
       }
    virtual ~SportsFrame(); {}
    void input();      // Get input characteristics for comparison.
    void eval();       // Evaluate the input characteristics.
    void output();     // Determine output behavior.
};
```

In Turbo Pascal:

```
type
SportsFramePointer = ^SportsFrame;    { a pointer to the frame }
                     { so you can create it dynamically with New }
SportsFrame = object(BaseFrame)
  Total_points : integer;        { this frame's characteristics }
  Points_against : integer;
  Wins : integer;
  Losses : integer;
  Cur_Tp : integer;                { input characteristics }
  Cur_Pa : integer;
  Cur_W : integer;
  Cur_L : integer;
  constructor Init(I1, I2, I3, I4 : integer);
                                { Create a SportsFrame. }
  destructor Done; virtual;     { Destroy a SportsFrame. }
  procedure Input; virtual;     { Get input. }
  procedure Eval; virtual;      { Evaluate input using the }
                                { SportsFrame's rule. }
  procedure Output; virtual;    { Determine output. }
end;
```

```
constructor SportsFrame.Init(I1, I2, I3, I4 : integer);
                                    { constructor implementation }
begin
  Total_points := I1;
  Points_against := I2;
  Wins := I3;
  Losses := I4;
end;

destructor SportsFrame.Done;      { destructor implementation }
begin
end;
```

SportsFrame has four characteristics — *Total_points*, *Points_against*, *Wins*, and *Losses* — but you can easily add more, either by adding variables to *SportsFrame* or by deriving a new type from *BaseFrame* (more on that later).

The current input (*Cur_Tp*, *Cur_Pa*, *Cur_W*, and *Cur_L*) is also encapsulated in *SportsFrame*, allowing each *SportsFrame* to have its own input. *BaseFrame* is general and could represent anything from a simple lookup system to an advisory system to a real-time system that receives input from devices. To create a gauge, for example, we might derive *GaugeFrame* from *BaseFrame* with variables to represent such characteristics as temperature, pressure, and flow.

We'll need to decide how to store and access each frame derived from *BaseFrame*. Remember, we want the system to be as flexible as it can be and to grow and evolve. The most flexible structure for handling unknown growth is a collection (a list, for example). Recall the one we created in Chapter 4. It began with a node consisting of pointers to the next node and to an instance of the base type or any type derived from the base. Next, we used the node to create a list of nodes. Each node on the list could accept a *BaseFrame* using the *Add(BaseFrame...)* behavior.

In this example, the base type is *BaseFrame*. In C++:

```
// Node and List

// A struct's characteristics are public by default.

struct Node {              // The list item can be BaseFrame or any
  BaseFrame *Item;         // class derived from BaseFrame.
  Node *Next;              // Point to next node type.
  Node(BaseFrame *F, Node *N) : Item = F; Next = N; {}
  ~Node() { delete Item;}
};

class List {               // The list of types pointed to by Nodes
  Node *Nodes;             // points to a node.
public:
  List(); { Nodes = NULL } // constructor
  ~List();                 // destructor
  void add(BaseFrame *NewItem);  // Add item; can be a BaseFrame
                                 // or a descendant of BaseFrame.
  void input();                  // Send input message to
                                 // BaseFrame.
  void report();                 // Send report message to
                                 // BaseFrame.
};
```

In Turbo Pascal:

```
{ Node and List }

type

{ In Turbo Pascal, an object's behaviors are public by default. }
NodePointer = ^Node;
Node = object              { The list item can be BaseFrame }
  Item : BaseFramePointer; { or any object derived from it. }
  Next : NodePointer;      { Point to next node type. }
  constructor Init(F : BaseFramePointer; N : NodePointer);
  destructor Done;         { Delete Item.}
end;
```

```
constructor Node.Init(F : BaseFramePointer; N : NodePointer);
begin
  Item := F;
  Next := N;
end;

destructor Node.Done;
begin
end;

type

List = object            { The list of types pointed to by }
  Nodes : NodePointer;    { Nodes points to a node. }
  constructor Init;
  destructor Done;        { Add an item to the list. }
  procedure Add(NewItem : BaseFramePointer);
  procedure Input;        { Input to items. }
  procedure Report;       { List the items. }
end;
```

The *List* method's implementation is shown at the end of the chapter in Listings 5-1 and 5-2.

Again, note that a C++ *struct* is a class with all its members public by default. All members of a class are normally private by default. By using C++'s access keywords, you can use *struct* and *class* interchangeably.

The three keys to making this system flexible are inheritance, which lets you modify *BaseFrame* by deriving new types from it; polymorphism, which lets the same name represent different behaviors; and dynamic memory allocation, which lets you create instances of *BaseFrame*s and types derived from *BaseFrame* at run time. The interface to the different implementations stays the same. In this example, *List* sends a message (*Report*), which in turn sends a message to each *BaseFrame* (or descendant of *BaseFrame*) to compare each descendant's characteristics to those coming into the system.

Report sends an evaluation message to each derived frame, which uses its own implementation of *eval* to decide the input. If the frame can't determine an output based on its characteristics, it outputs nothing and *Report* continues to traverse the list of frames derived from *BaseFrame*. In C++:

```
Node* Current = Nodes;

while (Current != NULL) {          // Do while we have BaseFrames.
  Current->Item->eval();           // Check rule for this node.
  Current = Current->Next;         // Point to the next node.
};
```

In Turbo Pascal:

```
var
  Current : NodePtr;
begin
  Current := Nodes;

  { Do while we have BaseFrames or descendants. }
  while (Current <> NIL) do
  begin
    Current^.Item^.eval;           { Check rule for this node. }
    Current := Current^.Next;      { Point to the next node. }
  end;
end;
```

The more general an object type, the easier it is to extend. The input, evaluation, and output methods for *BaseFrame* are all virtual, so you can derive new frames and reimplement any or all of a frame's behaviors.

In this example, *SportsFrame* implements its evaluation behavior in terms of an *and* rule. In other words, a *SportsFrame* produces an output if two of its existing characteristics match the current state of those characteristics. In C++:

```
void SportsFrame::eval() {                 // evaluation AND;
if ((Cur_Tp == Total_points)
  && (Cur_Pa == Points_against))
  output();
};
```

In Turbo Pascal:

```
procedure SportsFrame.Eval;                    { evaluation AND }
begin
if ((Cur_Tp = Total_points)
  and (Cur_Pa = Points_against))
then
  output;
end;
```

You can easily derive a new frame from *SportsFrame* to implement another rule (*or*, for example). In C++:

```
class OrFrame : public SportsFrame {
  public:
  OrFrame(int I1, int I2, int I3, int I4):
    SportsFrame(I1,I2,I3,I4){}
  void eval();
};

void OrFrame::eval() {                    // Implement OR.
  if ((Cur_Tp == Total_points)
      || (Cur_Pa == Points_against)
      || (Cur_W == Wins)
      || (Cur_L == Losses))
      output();
};
```

In Turbo Pascal:

```
type
OrFramePointer = ^OrFrame;
OrFrame = object(SportsFrame)
  constructor Init(I1, I2, I3, I4 : integer);
  destructor Done; virtual;
  procedure Eval; virtual;
end;

constructor OrFrame.Init(I1,I2,I3,I4 : integer);
begin
  SportsFrame.Init(I1,I2,I3,I4);
end;
```

150

```
destructor OrFrame.Done;
begin
end;

procedure OrFrame.Eval;      { Implement OR. }
begin
  if ((Cur_Tp = Total_points)
    or (Cur_Pa = Points_against)
    or (Cur_W = Wins)
    or (Cur_L = Losses))
  then
     output;
end;
```

You can add instances of *SportsFrame*s and *OrFrame*s to a single list (that is, a single system) and thus implement both *and* and *or* rules simultaneously. The following code constructs and adds two *SportsFrame*s and one *OrFrame* to the same list. In C++:

```
main() {
  // Declare a list (calls List constructor).
  List AList;

  // Create and add knowledge frames to a list.
  AList.add(new SportsFrame(75, 82, 1, 5));
  AList.add(new SportsFrame(51, 82, 6, 3));
  AList.add(new OrFrame(86, 84, 7, 2));
}
```

In Turbo Pascal:

```
var
  AList : List;
begin

  { Declare a list (calls List constructor). }
  AList.Init;

  { Create and add knowledge frames to a list. }
  AList.Add(New(SportsFramePointer,Init(75, 82, 1, 5)));
  AList.Add(New(SportsFramePointer,Init(51, 82, 6, 3)));
  AList.Add(New(OrFramePointer,Init(86, 84, 7, 2)));
end;
```

The following code sends input to *SportsFrames* and *OrFrames* on the list. It traverses the list, displaying and evaluating the system, to produce specific output. In C++:

```
// Input to BaseFrames and descendants.
AList.input();

// Traverse list, display frames in expert system, and evaluate.
AList.report();
```

In Turbo Pascal:

```
{ Input to BaseFrames and descendants. }
AList.Input;

{ Traverse list, display frames, and evaluate. }
AList.Report;
```

Programming for Change

Programs composed of object types are more powerful and flexible because of their built-in capacity for change. Object-oriented design anticipates the evolution of real-world systems and programs. Any program of even modest complexity will change, so anticipating change is a natural process.

Change can take two forms. External changes take place in the outside world. For the system to continue modeling the outside world accurately, it must be able to change. A simple example is adding new printers or graphics terminals to a system. Adding desktop publishing features to a word-processing program is more complicated. Most programming systems (particularly structured systems) assume that all changes are external.

Internal changes take place in your understanding of a problem. Nothing has necessarily changed in the outside world; rather, your perception of the problem has changed. For example, you might rewrite an algorithm to increase its execution speed or reorganize code to improve its readability. You might also discover that three different types have features in common and decide to create an abstract base type from which to derive them.

You may discover that you can improve a type you created for a program by modifying its design. Most non-object-oriented languages assume you understand the system completely before you begin coding and either won't make mistakes or won't learn from them. In short, non-object-oriented languages don't adapt easily to internal changes.

Object-oriented languages, on the other hand, provide techniques for creating systems that adapt easily to external or internal changes. Object-oriented design uses these techniques and thus lets you and your ideas grow with the system. You don't need to know everything about the system before you begin to code. Of course, you can never know *everything* about a system, yet that's exactly what most non-object-oriented languages require.

Complex projects, such as those associated with artificial intelligence, must be explorative, creative, dynamic, and experimental — requirements easily met by object-oriented languages.

Listing 5-1. *And/or* **frame-based expert system in C++.**

```
#include <iostream.h>              // for cout
#include <conio.h>

// class hierarchy

class BaseFrame {
public:
   BaseFrame(); {}
   virtual ~BaseFrame(); {}
   virtual void input(); {}        // Get input characteristics for
                                   // comparison.
   virtual void eval(); {}         // Evaluate input
                                   // characteristics.
   virtual void output(); {}       // Determine output behavior.
}
```

```
class SportsFrame : public BaseFrame {
public:
   int Total_points;
   int Points_against;
   int Wins;
   int Losses;
   int Cur_Tp;
   int Cur_Pa;
   int Cur_W;
   int Cur_L;

   SportsFrame(int I1, int I2, int I3, int I4)
     { Total_points = I1;
       Points_against = I2;
       Wins = I3;
       Losses = I4;
     }
   ~SportsFrame();
   void input();
   void eval();
   void output();
};

void Frame::input() {

   Cur_Tp    = 86;
   Cur_Pa    = 84;
   Cur_W     = 7;
   Cur_L     = 2;

   // Display current values.
    cout << "Current_Points = " << Cur_Tp << " ";
    cout << "Current_Against = " << Cur_Pa << " ";
    cout << "Current_Wins = " << Cur_W << " ";
    cout << "Current_Losses = " << Cur_L << "\n";
}

void SportsFrame::output() {

   cout << "Match!\n";
   // Implement specific output here.
};
```

```
void SportsFrame::eval() {        // evaluation AND;

if ((Cur_Tp == Total_points)
   && (Cur_Pa == Points_against))
   output();
};

class OrFrame : public SportsFrame {
   public:
   OrFrame(int I1, int I2, int I3, int I4):
     SportsFrame(I1,I2,I3,I4){}
   void eval();
};

void OrFrame::eval() {            // Implement OR.

   if ((Cur_Tp == Total_points)
      || (Cur_Pa == Points_against)
      || (Cur_W == Wins)
      || (Cur_L == Losses))
      output();
};

// Node and List

struct Node {               // The list item can be BaseFrame or any
   BaseFrame *Item;         // class derived from BaseFrame.
   Node *Next;              // Point to next node type.
   Node(BaseFrame *F, Node *N) : Item(F), Next(N) {}
   ~Node() { delete Item;}
};

class List {                // The list of types pointed to by Nodes
   Node *Nodes;             // points to a node.
public:
   List() : Nodes(NULL) {}      // constructor
   ~List();                     // destructor
   void add(BaseFrame *NewItem); // Add an item to the list.
   void input();                // Input to items.
   void report();               // List the items.
};
```

```
// member functions for List class
List::~List()                   // destructor
{
   while (Nodes) {              // until end of list
     Node *N = Nodes;           // Get node pointed to.
     Nodes = Nodes->Next;       // Point to next node.
     delete N;                  // Delete pointer's memory.
   };
}

void List::add(BaseFrame *NewItem)
{
   Nodes = new Node(NewItem, Nodes);
}

void List::input() {
   Node* Current = Nodes;
   while (Current) {
     Current->Item->input();
     Current = Current->Next;
   }
}

void List::report()
{
   Node *Current = Nodes;
   while (Current)
   {
     // Display Total_points of item in current node.
     cout << "Total_points = " <<
     Current->Item->Total_points << " ";

     // Display Points_against of item in current node.
     cout << "Points_against = " <<
     Current->Item->Points_against << " ";

     // Display Wins of item in current node.
     cout << "Wins = " << Current->Item->Wins << " ";

     // Display Losses of item in current node.
     cout << "Losses = " << Current->Item->Losses << "\n";
```

```
      // Evaluate this node.
      Current->Item->eval();

      // Point to the next node.
      Current = Current->Next;
   };
}

// main program
main()
{
   // Declare a list (calls List constructor).
   List AList;

   // Create and add knowledge frames to a list.
   AList.add(new SportsFrame(75, 82, 1, 5));
   AList.add(new SportsFrame(51, 82, 6, 3));
   AList.add(new OrFrame(86, 84, 7, 2));

   // Input to BaseFrames and descendants.
   AList.input();

   // Traverse list, display frames in expert system, and
   // evaluate.
   AList.report();

   getch();                        // Wait for a keypress.
}
```

Listing 5-2. *And/or* frame-based expert system in Turbo Pascal.

```
{ object hierarchy }
type

BaseFramePtr : ^BaseFrame;
BaseFrame = object
   constructor Init;
   destructor Done; virtual;
   procedure Input; virtual;      { Get input. }
   procedure Eval; virtual;       { Evaluate input using derived }
                                  { frame's rule. }
```

```pascal
      procedure Output;virtual;      { Determine output. }
   end;

SportsFramePointer = ^SportsFrame;
SportsFrame = object
   Total_points : integer;
   Points_against : integer;
   Wins : integer;
   Losses : integer;
   Cur_Tp : integer;
   Cur_Pa : integer;
   Cur_W : integer;
   Cur_L : integer;
   constructor Init(I1, I2, I3, I4 : integer);
   destructor Done; virtual;
   procedure Input;
   procedure Eval; virtual;
   procedure Output;
end;

constructor BaseFrame.Init;
begin
end;

destructor BaseFrame Done;
begin
end;

procedure BaseFrame.Input;
begin
end;

procedure BaseFrame.Eval;
begin
end;

procedure BaseFrame.Output;
begin
end;
```

```
constructor SportsFrame.Init(I1, I2, I3, I4 : integer);
begin
    Total_points := I1;
    Points_against := I2;
    Wins := I3;
    Losses := I4;
end;

destructor SportsFrame.Done;
begin
end;

procedure SportsFrame.Input;
begin

    Cur_Tp    := 86;
    Cur_Pa    := 84;
    Cur_W     :=  7;
    Cur_L     :=  2;

    { Display field values of item in current node. }
    Write('Current_Points = ', Cur_Tp, ' ');
    Write('Current_Against = ',Cur_Pa, ' ');
    Write('Current_Wins = ',Cur_W,' ');
    Writeln('Current_Losses = ',Cur_L);
end;

procedure SportsFrame.Output;
begin
    Writeln('Match!');
    { Implement specific output here. }
end;

procedure SportsFrame.Eval;                 { evaluation AND }
begin

if ((Cur_Tp = Total_points)
    and (Cur_Pa = Points_against))
then
    output;
end;
```

```
type

OrFramePointer = ^OrFrame;
OrFrame = object(SportsFrame)
    constructor Init(I1, I2, I3, I4 : integer);
    destructor Done; virtual;
    procedure Eval; virtual;
end;

constructor OrFrame.Init(I1,I2,I3,I4 : integer);
begin
    SportsFrame.Init(I1,I2,I3,I4);
end;

destructor OrFrame.Done;
begin
end;

procedure OrFrame.Eval;                     { Implement OR. }
begin
    if ((Cur_Tp = Total_points)
      or (Cur_Pa = Points_against)
      or (Cur_W = Wins)
      or (Cur_L = Losses))
    then
      output;
end;

{ Node and List }

type

NodePointer = ^Node;
Node = object                    { The list item can be }
    Item : BaseFramePointer;     { BaseFrame or descendants. }
    Next : NodePointer;          { Point to next node type }
    constructor Init(F : BaseFramePointer; N : NodePointer);
    destructor Done;             { Delete Item.}
end;
```

```
constructor Node.Init(F : BaseFramePointer; N : NodePointer);
begin
    Item := F;
    Next := N;
end;

destructor Node.Done;
begin
end;

type

List = object                     { The list of types pointed to }
    Nodes : NodePointer;          { by Nodes points to a node. }
    constructor Init;
    destructor Done;              { Add an item to the list. }
    procedure Add(NewItem : BaseFramePointer);
    procedure Input;              { Input to items. }
    procedure Report;             { List the items. }
end;

{ methods for List }
constructor List.Init;
begin
    Nodes := NIL;
end;

destructor List.Done;
var
    N : NodePointer;
begin
    while (Nodes <> NIL) do        { until end of list }
    begin
      N := Nodes;                  { Get node pointed to. }
      Nodes := Nodes^.Next;        { Point to next node. }
      dispose(N);                  { Delete pointer's memory. }
    end;
end;
```

```
procedure List.Add(NewItem : BaseFramePointer);
var
    N : NodePointer;
begin
    New(N); N^.Item := NewItem;
    N^.Next := Nodes;
    Nodes := N;
end;

procedure List.Input;
var
    Current : NodePointer;
begin
    Current := Nodes;
    while (Current <> nil) do
    begin
      Current^.Item^.Input;
      Current := Current^.Next;
    end;
end;

procedure List.Report;
var
    Current : NodePointer;
begin
    Current := Nodes;
    while (Current <> nil) do
    begin
      { Display Total_points of item in current node. }
      Write('Total_points = ',Current^.Item^.Total_points,' ');

      { Display Points_against of item in current node. }
      Write('Points_against = ',Current^.Item^.Points_against,' ');

      { Display Wins of item in current node. }
      Write('Wins = ',Current^.Item^.Wins,' ');

      { Display Losses of item in current node. }
      Writeln('Losses = ',Current^.Item^.Losses);

      { Evaluate this node. }
      Current^.Item^.Eval;
```

```
      { Point to the next node. }
      Current := Current^.Next;
    end;
end;

{ main program }
var
   AList : List;
begin

   { Declare a list (calls List constructor). }
   AList.Init;

   { Create and add knowledge frames to a list. }
   AList.Add(new(SportsFramePointer,Init(75, 82, 1, 5)));
   AList.Add(new(SportsFramePointer,Init(51, 82, 6, 3)));
   AList.Add(new(OrFramePointer,Init(86, 84, 7, 2)));

   { Input to BaseFrames and descendants. }
   AList.Input;

   { Traverse list, display frames, and evaluate. }
   AList.Report;

   Readln;                        { Wait for a keypress. }
end.
```

CHAPTER 6

An Object-Oriented Neural Network

If you want to shrink something, you must first allow it to expand. If you want to take something, you must first allow it to be given. This is called the subtle perception of the way things are.
— *Lao-tzu*

Not even our technological evolution has been a linear movement from lower to higher levels, but rather a process punctuated by massive regressions.
— *Riane Eisler*

Object-oriented techniques make it easier to represent the world in programming models. Ideally, a user-defined type in a program corresponds to a type in the world you want to represent. Thus, finding or discovering types is your first task in object-oriented programming.

If you describe a problem or system in terms of object types and build programs out of those objects, the programs will be easier to maintain and revise. As the problem or system changes, you revise or reimplement an object to correspond to those changes. The act of revision becomes an act of extension rather than reconceptualization.

In recent years, computers have become the preeminent representational (or modeling) tool. An excellent example of how scientists use computers to represent an aspect of the world is the neural network, which attempts to capture aspects of how we believe the brain works.

A neural network is a dynamic system consisting of layers of neurons connected to each other. Each neuron's state is determined by the messages sent to it by all the neurons connected to it. These messages tell the neuron the state of each neuron sending a message and the weight (or strength) of the connection between them. In most commercial neural network systems on the PC, the neurons in one layer connect only to the neurons in immediately adjoining layers. Neurons within a layer don't connect to each other.

Each layer of neurons can be one of three types:

- An input layer consisting of a pattern to classify or match, a problem to solve, and so on
- A hidden layer — the network's internal representation of connections
- An output layer — a resulting classification, pattern, or solution.

In most neural network models, all the neurons in a single input layer are connected to all the neurons in a hidden layer; all the neurons in the hidden layer are connected to all the neurons in an output layer (see Figure 6-1). A neural network can have more than one hidden layer, but the connection scheme is similar — the neurons in the second hidden layer are connected to the neurons in both the first hidden layer and the output layer.

A neuron is always in one of two states: on or off. The combined, weighted states of all the neurons connected to a neuron determine its state. The neurons in the input layer are connected to sources (devices or a program) outside the network, and the initial states of these neurons are determined by the messages sent to them from the outside world.

The states of neurons in the hidden layer are determined by the messages sent by neurons in the input layer; the states of neurons in the output layer are determined by the messages sent from the hidden layer. These messages are determined by several factors: the network model that calculates the weights of inputs, an activation function, and a transfer function. Figure 6-2 illustrates how input messages generally produce output messages in these neural network models.

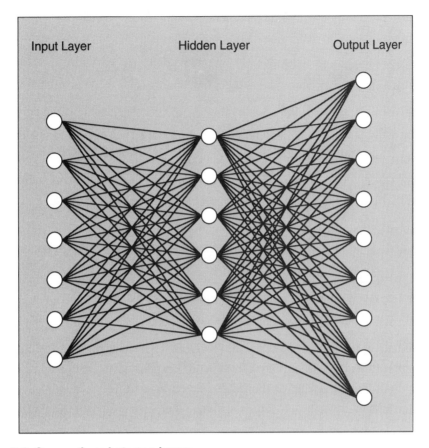

Figure 6-1. Connections between layers.

When messages have been sent to all the output neurons in the network, the network has reached a temporary state. The network then evaluates its state (by comparing it to some desired state) to determine how much error it contains. The total error in the network is equal to the sum of the errors in individual neurons and determines what the network does next.

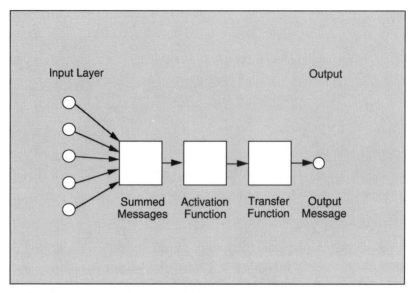

Figure 6-2. Input messages generally produce output messages.

For example, if a back-propagation network finds the error too large, it sends a message back through the network from neuron to neuron (to the hidden layer, back to the input layer, forward to the hidden layer, then on to the output layer). The message tells every neuron to adjust itself and therefore reduce the total error in the network. For more information about specific neural networks, check the reference list (Appendix B).

Once the network has looped back to the output layer, it recalculates its error. It eventually settles into a stable state and sends an output message identifying that state. This output signal is the solution to the problem the network is trying to solve.

Neural networks are information processors that are based on mathematical models of how we think the brain works. Although they are similar to expert systems in that they solve (or classify) a new problem by matching its characteristics to an existing problem, they differ in two important ways: Expert systems use rules to generate output, while neural networks use examples; expert systems require complete information, while neural networks can produce results from incomplete information.

Because neural network technology is new and still evolving, researchers haven't yet agreed on an ideal model. In fact, research takes place all over the world, much of it in isolation; different premises and goals and distinct approaches to developing models continue to appear and evolve.

In general, though, these neural network models share many related characteristics, making them suitable for development using object-oriented techniques. The idea is to describe the features of a neural network abstractly and derive new networks from the abstract type.

This chapter describes an abstract neural network to illustrate how complex problems in the world can be visualized more clearly as object types, then shows how you might use this neural network to derive other networks.

Neural networks are most often used for applications that involve some form of learning through repetition. You can build large networks that learn to repeat patterns based on large volumes of input. For example, you could create a neural network that predicted stock prices based on certain key economic indicators. If you then fed the network large volumes of data on past performance and historical stock prices, it would adapt and organize itself so that it could be used to estimate future stock prices.

Objects and Networks

First, let's try to find the objects that will describe the characteristics of a neural network. At this stage, you should think primarily about the boundaries of the object type and the gross interactions between types. The details of the network, such as how specific methods will be implemented, should be of less concern. Focus on external factors, those that determine the connections and interactions between types and the world outside the system.

Don't be overly concerned about methods at first; just concentrate on the object. Look for aspects of the system that might be duplicated, and try to find the smallest units first. If you're feeling imaginative, try to visualize how an object type will fit into the bigger picture and how it might adapt to change.

The smallest unit in a neural network is a neuron, which has a state and the ability to send messages to and receive messages from the neurons to which it's connected. The state of a neuron is determined by messages from other neurons. Connections have weights, and neurons change state by comparing the incoming message to a value determined by an activation function. If the message exceeds a certain value, the neuron is in an on, or 1, state. If not, the neuron is in an off, or 0, state.

A neuron's state is determined by its connections to adjoining neurons. Each neuron receiving a message turns itself on or off depending on the message. Typically, a message consists of a value determined by a function (for example, "weight times state").

After all the neurons have received messages and changed states accordingly, the network asks itself whether its current state is stable. It determines its status by comparing it to a value determined by an error function. If its state is within some error range, the network sends a message to the system stating that. If its state isn't stable enough, the network adjusts it and sends messages back through the network, changing the states of neurons until it settles into an acceptable state.

Each neural network model has its own methods, equations, connection schemes, activation functions, and so on for determining its state and stability; however, all networks share the characteristics just described.

Beginning with data, you might ask the following questions:

- How many patterns will be input to the network?
- How many neurons will be in each layer?
- How many layers will there be?
- How do we describe error, learning rates, and so on?
- How do we describe connection weights?

In C++, the characteristics of any neural network type might look like this:

```
class BaseNet {          // a basic neural network type
                         // Includes matrix methods.
public:
   float Eta,            // default learning rate
         Alpha,          // default momentum factor
         ErrorLevel,     // acceptable error level
         Error;          // latest sum squared error value
   int   ErrorFreq,      // error reporting frequency
         nInputNodes,    // number of input nodes
         nHiddenNodes,   // number of hidden nodes
         nOutputNodes,   // number of output nodes
         nIterations,    // number of iterations
         nPatterns,      // number of patterns
         nRuns,          // number of runs or input lines
         H,              // index hidden layer
         I,              // index input layer
         J,              // index output layer
         P,              // index pattern number
         Q,              // index iteration number
         R;              // index run number
};
```

In Turbo Pascal:

```
BaseNet = object        { a basic neural network type }
                        { Includes matrix methods. }
   Eta,                 { default learning rate }
   Alpha,               { default momentum factor }
   ErrorLevel,          { acceptable error level }
   Error : real;        { latest sum squared error value }
   ErrorFreq,           { error reporting frequency }
   nInputNodes,         { number of input nodes }
   nHiddenNodes,        { number of hidden nodes }
   nOutputNodes,        { number of output nodes }
   nIterations,         { number of iterations }
   nPatterns,           { number of patterns }
   nRuns,               { number of runs or input lines }
   H,                   { index hidden layer }
   I,                   { index input layer }
   J,                   { index output layer }
```

```
    P,                      { index pattern number }
    Q,                      { index iteration number }
    R  : integer;           { index run number }
end;
```

In addition to having those characteristics, a network needs to create itself and initialize default values, load weights, and other information (probably from a file), iterate itself (for training and problem classification), and delete itself when it's no longer needed.

You need to specify where the information to the network comes from and where the network will send its output message (its interactions with the outside world). Once the network gets started, it will generate its own messages.

You must also specify how the network will calculate, store, and update error information and other data. Neural networks usually use a matrix to store this information.

Because a few characteristics will differ from one network to another and the iteration loop will differ substantially, you should make this loop a virtual method. Each network can then implement it as it sees fit.

The base type for any neural network, with the additions mentioned earlier, might look like this in C++:

```
class BaseNet {            // a basic neural network type
                           // Includes matrix methods.
public:
    float Eta,             // default learning rate
          Alpha,           // default momentum factor
          ErrorLevel,      // acceptable error level
          Error;           // latest sum squared error value
    int   ErrorFreq,       // error reporting frequency
          nInputNodes,     // number of input nodes
          nHiddenNodes,    // number of hidden nodes
          nOutputNodes,    // number of output nodes
          nIterations,     // number of iterations
          nPatterns,       // number of patterns
          nRuns,           // number of runs or input lines
```

```
            H,              // index hidden layer
            I,              // index input layer
            J,              // index output layer
            P,              // index pattern number
            Q,              // index iteration number
            R;              // index run number
    FILE    *RunFile,       // run file
            *PatternFile,   // source pattern input file
            *WeightsInFile, // initial weight file
            *WeightsOutFile,// final weight output file
            *ResultsFile,   // results output file
            *ErrorFile;     // error output file
    char KeyboardRequest;   // true when key pressed
    char szResults[40];     // various file names
    char szError[40];
    char szPattern[40];
    char szWeights[40];
    char szWeightsOut[40];


// matrix
// typedefs and prototypes for dynamic storage of arrays
    typedef float *FLOATPTR;      // pointer to a real
    typedef FLOATPTR VECTOR;      // a vector: one column
    typedef FLOATPTR *MATRIX;     // a matrix: two columns


// network layers
// arrays for inputs, outputs, deltas, weights, and target outputs
    MATRIX  Out0;           // input layer
    MATRIX  Out1;           // hidden layer
    MATRIX  Delta1;         // delta at hidden layer
    MATRIX  Delw1;          // change in weight from input to hidden
    MATRIX  W1;             // weights input:hidden
    MATRIX  Out2;           // output layer
    MATRIX  Delta2;         // delta at output layer
    MATRIX  Delw2;          // weights hidden:output
    MATRIX  W2;             // weights hidden:output
    MATRIX  TargetOutput;   // target output
    VECTOR  PatternID;      // identifier for each stored pattern


// memory allocation methods
    void  AllocateVector(VECTOR *Vector, int nCols);
    void  AllocateColumns(FLOATPTR Matrix[], int nRows, int nCols);
```

```
    void  AllocateMatrix(MATRIX *pmatrix, int nRows, int nCols);
    void  FreeMatrix(MATRIX Matrix, int nRows);
    BaseNet();                              // constructor
    ~BaseNet() {};                          // destructor
    virtual void Iterate(char Netname) {};// abstract iteration
                                            // loop for any network
};
```

and like this in Turbo Pascal:

```
type
    FLOATPTR : ^real;       { pointer to a real }
    VECTOR   : FLOATPTR;    { a vector: one column }
    MATRIX   : FLOATPTR;    { a matrix: two columns }
    MATRIXPTR: ^MATRIX;     { pointer to a matrix }
    VECTORPTR: ^VECTOR;     { pointer to a vector }

BaseNet = object           { a basic neural network type }
                           { Includes matrix methods. }

    Eta,                   { default learning rate }
    Alpha,                 { default momentum factor }
    ErrorLevel,            { acceptable error level }
    Error : real;          { latest sum squared error value }
    ErrorFreq,             { error reporting frequency }
    nInputNodes,           { number of input nodes }
    nHiddenNodes,          { number of hidden nodes }
    nOutputNodes,          { number of output nodes }
    nIterations,           { number of iterations }
    nPatterns,             { number of patterns }
    nRuns,                 { number of runs or input lines }
    H,                     { index hidden layer }
    I,                     { index input layer }
    J,                     { index output layer }
    P,                     { index pattern number }
    Q,                     { index iteration number }
    R  : integer;          { index run number }
    RunFile,               { run file }
    PatternFile,           { source pattern input file }
    WeightsInFile,         { initial weight file }
    WeightsOutFile,        { final weight output file }
    ResultsFile,           { results output file }
    ErrorFile : File;      { error output file }
```

```
    KeyboardRequest : char; { true when key pressed }
    szResults : string[40]; { various file names }
    szError : string[40];
    szPattern : string[40];
    szWeights : string[40];
    szWeightsOut : string[40];

{ matrix }
{ network layers }
{ arrays for inputs, outputs, deltas, weights, target outputs }
    Out0,                       { input layer }
    Out1,                       { hidden layer }
    Delta1,                     { delta at hidden layer }
    Delw1,                      { change in weights input:hidden }
    W1,                         { weights input:hidden }
    Out2,                       { output layer }
    Delta2,                     { delta at output layer }
    Delw2,                      { change in weights hidden:output }
    W2,                         { weights hidden:output }
    TargetOutput : MATRIX;      { target output }
    PatternID    : VECTOR;      { identifier for each stored pattern }

{ memory allocation methods }
    procedure AllocateVector(AVector : VECTORPTR; nCols : integer);
    procedure AllocateColumns(AColumn : FLOATPTR; nRows : integer;
                        nCols : integer);
    procedure AllocateMatrix(Pmatrix : MATRIXPTR; nRows : integer;
                        nCols : integer);
    procedure FreeMatrix(AMatrix : MATRIX; nRows : integer);
    constructor Init;           { constructor }
    destructor Done;            { destructor }
    procedure Iterate(Netname : char); virtual;
                        { abstract iteration loop for any }
                        { network }
end;
```

The BaseNet constructor initializes a network's default fields. In C++:

```
BaseNet::BaseNet() {
    Eta  = 0.15,           // default learning rate
    Alpha = 0.075;         // default momentum factor
```

```
    ErrorFreq = 100;          // error reporting frequency
    ErrorLevel = 0.04;        // acceptable error level
    KeyboardRequest = 0;      // true when key pressed
};
```

In Turbo Pascal:

```
constructor BaseNet.Init
    Eta    :=  0.15,          { default learning rate }
    Alpha :=  0.075;          { default momentum factor }
    ErrorFreq := 100;         { error reporting frequency }
    ErrorLevel := 0.04;       { acceptable error level }
    KeyboardRequest := 0;     { true when key pressed }
end;
```

Deriving New Networks

The characteristics just described are part of most neural networks. Thus, this generic neural network could serve as the base type for a group of related neural networks.

For example, you could derive a back-propagation neural network from this base type by reconstructing the base network and implementing a new *Iterate* method. In C++:

```
class BackProp : public BaseNet {      // back-propagation
public:                                 // network
    BackProp() {};
    ~BackProp() {};
    void Iterate(char Netname);         // specific iteration loop
};                                      // for this network
```

In Turbo Pascal:

```
BackProp = object(BaseNet)         { back-propagation network }
    constructor Init;
    destructor Done; virtual;
    procedure Iterate(Netname : char); virtual;
                                   { specific iteration loop }
    end;                           { for this network }
```

Many other networks can use the characteristics of *BaseNet*. In general, deriving a new network means adding a few data fields and implementing the *Iteration* method. A self-organizing neural network might look like this in C++:

```
class SelfOrganizing : public BaseNet {
    int Kohonen_units;      // specific units for calculating
    int Grossberg_units;    // error in this network
public:
    SelfOrganizing();       // Construct this neural network.
    ~SelfOrganizing();      // Clean up this network.
    void Iterate();         // Implement specific iteration loop.
};
```

and like this in Turbo Pascal:

```
SelfOrganizing = object(BaseNet)
    int Kohonen_units;              { units for calculating error }
    int Grossberg_units;
    constructor Init;               { Construct neural network. }
    destructor Done; virtual;       { Clean up this network. }
    procedure Iterate; virtual;     { Implement iteration loop. }
end;
```

Data Lists and Events

In describing a generic neural network, we focused on the network's characteristics, behaviors, and interactions with the outside world. Its characteristics consist of the information it needs to know or remember, its behaviors are what it needs to do, and its interactions with the outside world are its responses and stimuli. The network's operation consists of the messages exchanged by neurons.

The base network in this example might not yet be a perfect type, but it's a good start. If you see something that needs to be changed, you can change it. The base network isn't too large (a good sign) or too complex (another good sign) and is abstract enough to allow many kinds of networks to be derived from it. Listing 6-1, for example, shows a complete back-propagation neural network derived from the *BaseNet* neural network object.

For systems such as this one, a good starting point for discovering object types is the data. Other systems might be primarily event-driven or even function-driven. The beauty of object-oriented programming is that you can approach the discovery of object types from any direction, at any level, depending on the needs of the project. The types are more important than the approach.

Object-oriented programming encourages us to personalize and experiment with programs. We write programs by discovering, implementing, and deriving new types from existing ones. Maintaining and extending programs is an ongoing process, and object-oriented programming makes it easier to do both.

The next chapter uses the techniques discussed so far to suggest a design philosophy that will help you think in object types. Be forewarned, however, that an object-oriented philosophy can only be expected to evolve and expand as the world and our ideas about the world change.

Listing 6-1. Back-propagation neural network.

```
// C++ object-oriented base neural network and derived back-
// propagation neural network based on the equations in
// Rummelhart and McClelland's Parallel Distributed
// Processing and the shareware back-propagation neural
// network written in C by Eberhart and Dobbins and
// published in Micro Cornucopia (Jan./Feb. 1990).

#include <stdio.h>
#include <stdlib.h>
#include <math.h>
#include <conio.h>
#include <ctype.h>
#include <string.h>
#include <iostream.h>

#define ESC 27
#define ITEMS 8

// object types
class BaseNet {            // a basic neural network type
                           // Includes matrix methods.
```

```
public:
    float Eta,              // default learning rate
          Alpha,            // default momentum factor
          ErrorLevel,       // acceptable error level
          Error;            // latest sum squared error value
    char  KeyboardRequest;  // true when key pressed
    int   ErrorFreq,        // error reporting frequency
          nInputNodes,      // number of input nodes
          nHiddenNodes,     // number of hidden nodes
          nOutputNodes,     // number of output nodes
          nIterations,      // number of iterations
          nPatterns,        // number of patterns
          nRuns,            // number of runs or input lines
          H,                // index hidden layer
          I,                // index input layer
          J,                // index output layer
          P,                // index pattern number
          Q,                // index iteration number
          R;                // index run number
    FILE  *RunFile,         // run file
          *PatternFile,     // source pattern input file
          *WeightsInFile,   // initial weight file
          *WeightsOutFile,  // final weight output file
          *ResultsFile,     // results output file
          *ErrorFile;       // error output file
    char  szResults[40];    // various file names
    char  szError[40];
    char  szPattern[40];
    char  szWeights[40];
    char  szWeightsOut[40];

// matrix
// typedefs and prototypes for dynamic storage of arrays
    typedef  float *FLOATPTR;    // pointer to a real
    typedef  FLOATPTR VECTOR;    // a vector: one column
    typedef  FLOATPTR *MATRIX;   // a matrix: two columns

// network layers
// arrays for inputs, outputs, deltas, weights, and target outputs
    MATRIX  Out0;           // input layer
    MATRIX  Out1;           // hidden layer
    MATRIX  Delta1;         // delta at hidden layer
```

```
    MATRIX  Delw1;              // change in weights input:hidden
    MATRIX  W1;                 // weights input:hidden
    MATRIX  Out2;               // output layer
    MATRIX  Delta2;             // delta at output layer
    MATRIX  Delw2;              // change in weights
                                // hidden:output
    MATRIX  W2;                 // weights hidden:output
    MATRIX  TargetOutput;       // target output
    VECTOR  PatternID;          // identifier for each stored
                                // pattern

// memory allocation methods
    void  AllocateVector(VECTOR *Vector, int nCols);
    void  AllocateColumns(FLOATPTR Matrix[], int nRows, int nCols);
    void  AllocateMatrix(MATRIX *pmatrix, int nRows, int nCols);
    void  FreeMatrix(MATRIX Matrix, int nRows);

    BaseNet();                  // constructor
    ~BaseNet() {};              // destructor
    virtual void Iterate(char Netname) {};// abstract iteration
                                        // loop for any network
};

class BackProp : public BaseNet {     // back-propagation
public:                               // network
    BackProp() {};
    ~BackProp() {};
    void Iterate(char Netname);    // iteration loop for this
};                                 //  network

// BaseNet constructor initializes default fields.

BaseNet::BaseNet() {
    Eta   = 0.15,               // default learning rate
    Alpha = 0.075;              // default momentum factor
    ErrorFreq = 100;            // error reporting frequency
    ErrorLevel = 0.04;          // acceptable error level
    KeyboardRequest = 0;        // true when key pressed
};
```

```
// BaseNet methods

// implementation of array allocation routines
// Allocate space for a vector of float cells, a one-dimensional
// dynamic vector[cols].

void BaseNet::AllocateVector(VECTOR *Vector, int nCols)
{
   if ((*Vector = (VECTOR) calloc(nCols, sizeof(float))) == NULL)
   {
     cout << " Not enough memory!\n";   // If not, abort.
     exit(1);
   }
}

// Allocate space for dynamic, two-dimensional matrix[rows][cols].
void BaseNet::AllocateColumns(FLOATPTR Matrix[], int nRows,
     int nCols)
{
   int i;
   for (i = 0; i < nRows; i++)
     AllocateVector(&Matrix[i], nCols);
}

void BaseNet::AllocateMatrix(MATRIX *Pmatrix, int nRows,
     int nCols)
{
   if ((*Pmatrix = (MATRIX) calloc(nRows, sizeof(FLOATPTR))) ==
       NULL)
   {
     cout << "Not enough memory!\n";
     exit(1);
   }
   AllocateColumns(*Pmatrix, nRows, nCols);
};

// Free the memory used by the matrix.
void BaseNet::FreeMatrix(MATRIX Matrix, int nRows)
```

```
{
    int i;
    for (i = 0; i < nRows; i++)
      free(Matrix[i]);
    free(Matrix);
}
```

```
// specific implementation of iteration loop for a back-
// propagation network

void BackProp::Iterate(char Netname) {
    for (R = 0; R < nRuns; R++)
    {
      // Read and parse the run specification line to obtain
      // information about this network.
      fscanf(RunFile,
        "%s %s %s %s %s %d %d %d %d %d %f %f",
        szResults,                 // output results file
        szError,                   // error output file
        szPattern,                 // pattern input file
        szWeights,                 // initial weights file
        szWeightsOut,              // final weights output file
        &nPatterns,                // number of patterns to learn
        &nIterations,              // number of iterations through
                                   //  the data
        &nInputNodes,              // number of input nodes
        &nHiddenNodes,             // number of hidden nodes
        &nOutputNodes,             // number of output nodes
        &Eta,                      // learning rate
        &Alpha);                   // momentum factor

// Allocate dynamic storage for nodes and patterns.
    AllocateMatrix(&Out0,   nPatterns,    nInputNodes);
    AllocateMatrix(&Out1,   nPatterns,    nHiddenNodes);
    AllocateMatrix(&Out2,   nPatterns,    nOutputNodes);
    AllocateMatrix(&Delta2, nPatterns,    nOutputNodes);
    AllocateMatrix(&Delw2,  nOutputNodes, nHiddenNodes + 1);
    AllocateMatrix(&W2,     nOutputNodes, nHiddenNodes + 1);
    AllocateMatrix(&Delta1, nPatterns,    nHiddenNodes);
    AllocateMatrix(&Delw1,  nHiddenNodes, nInputNodes + 1);
    AllocateMatrix(&W1,     nHiddenNodes, nInputNodes + 1);
    AllocateMatrix(&TargetOutput,nPatterns, nOutputNodes);
    AllocateVector(&PatternID, nPatterns);
```

```
//  Read the initial weight matrices.
   if ((WeightsInFile = fopen(szWeights,"r")) == NULL)
   {
     cout << " Can't open file \n" << Netname << szWeights;
     exit(1);
   }

// Read input:hidden weights.
   for (H = 0;  H < nHiddenNodes;  H++)
     for (I = 0; I <= nInputNodes; I++)
     {
       fscanf(WeightsInFile, "%f", &W1[H][I]);
       Delw1[H][I] = 0.0;
     }

// Read hidden:out weights.
   for (J = 0;  J < nOutputNodes;  J++)
     for (H = 0; H <= nHiddenNodes; H++)
     {
       fscanf(WeightsInFile, "%f", &W2[J][H]);
       Delw2[J][H] = 0.0;
     }
   fclose(WeightsInFile);

// Read in all patterns to be learned.
   if ((PatternFile = fopen(szPattern, "r")) == NULL)
   {
     cout << " Can't open file \n" << Netname << szPattern;
     exit(1);
   }

   for (P = 0; P < nPatterns; P++)
   {
     for (I = 0; I < nInputNodes; I++)
       if (fscanf(PatternFile,"%f", &Out0[P][I])!= 1)
         goto AllPatternsRead;

// Read in target outputs for input patterns.
   for (J = 0; J < nOutputNodes; J++)
     fscanf(PatternFile, "%f", &TargetOutput[P][J]);
```

```
// Read in identifier for each pattern.
   fscanf(PatternFile, "%f ", &PatternID[P]);
   }
   AllPatternsRead:
   fclose(PatternFile);

   if (P < nPatterns)
   {
     cout << " Can't open file \n" << Netname << P << nPatterns;
     nPatterns = P;
   }

// Open error output file.
   if ((ErrorFile = fopen(szError, "w")) == NULL)
   {
     cout << " Can't open file \n" << Netname << szError;
     exit(1);
   }
   fprintf(stderr, nIterations > 1 ? "Training...\n" :
     "Testing\n");

// iteration loop
   for (Q = 0; Q < nIterations; Q++)
   {
     for (P = 0; P < nPatterns; P++)
     {

// hidden layer
// Sum input to hidden layer over all input-weight
// combinations.
     for (H = 0; H < nHiddenNodes; H++)
     {
       float Sum = W1[H][nInputNodes];  // Begin with bias.
       for (I = 0; I < nInputNodes; I++)
         Sum    +=   W1[H][I]  *  Out0[P][I];
       // Compute output using sigmoid function.
       Out1[P][H] = 1.0 / (1.0 + exp(-Sum));
     }
```

```
// output layer
  for (J = 0; J < nOutputNodes; J++)
  {
    float Sum = W2[J][nHiddenNodes];
    for (H = 0; H < nHiddenNodes; H++)
      Sum += W2[J][H] * Out1[P][H];
    // Compute output using sigmoid function.
    Out2[P][J] = 1.0 / (1.0 + exp(-Sum));
  }

  // delta output
  // Calculate deltas for each output unit for each pattern.
    for (J = 0;  J < nOutputNodes;  J++)
      Delta2[P][J] = (TargetOutput[P][J] - Out2[P][J])  *
                      Out2[P][J] * (1.0 - Out2[P][J]);

  // delta hidden
    for (H = 0; H < nHiddenNodes; H++)
    {
      float Sum = 0.0;
      for (J = 0; J < nOutputNodes; J++)
        Sum += Delta2[P][J] * W2[J][H];
      // Compute output using sigmoid function.
      Delta1[P][H] = Sum * Out1[P][H] * (1.0 - Out1[P][H]);
    }
  }

  // Adapt weights hidden:output
    for (J = 0; J < nOutputNodes; J++)
    {
      float Dw;                            // delta weight
      float Sum = 0.0;

  // sum of deltas for each output node for one epoch
  for (P = 0; P < nPatterns; P++)
    Sum  +=  Delta2[P][J];

  // Calculate new bias weight for each output unit.
  Dw = Eta * Sum + Alpha * Delw2[J][nHiddenNodes];
  W2[J][nHiddenNodes] += Dw;
  Delw2[J][nHiddenNodes] = Dw;            // delta for bias
```

```
// Calculate new weights.
for (H = 0; H < nHiddenNodes; H++)
{
   float Sum = 0.0;
   for (P = 0; P < nPatterns; P++)
     Sum  +=  Delta2[P][J] * Out1[P][H];
   Dw  =  Eta * Sum  +  Alpha * Delw2[J][H];
   W2[J][H]     +=   Dw;
   Delw2[J][H]  =  Dw;
}
}


// Adapt weights input:hidden.
for (H = 0; H < nHiddenNodes; H++)
{
   float Dw;              // delta weight
   float Sum = 0.0;
   for (P = 0; P < nPatterns; P++)
     Sum  +=  Delta1[P][H];

// Calculate new bias weight for each hidden unit.
Dw = Eta * Sum + Alpha * Delw1[H][nInputNodes];
W1[H][nInputNodes]    += Dw;
Delw1[H][nInputNodes] = Dw;

// Calculate new weights.
for (I = 0; I < nInputNodes; I++)
{
   float Sum = 0.0;
   for (P = 0; P < nPatterns; P++)
     Sum += Delta1[P][H] * Out0[P][I];
   Dw = Eta * Sum + Alpha * Delw1[H][I];
   W1[H][I] += Dw;
   Delw1[H][I] = Dw;
}
}
```

```
// Watch for keyboard requests.
   if (kbhit())
   {
     int c = getch();
     if ((c = toupper(c)) == 'E')
       KeyboardRequest++;
     else if (c == ESC)
       break;                            // End if ESC request.
   }

// Sum squared error.
   if (KeyboardRequest || (Q % ErrorFreq == 0))
   {
     for (P = 0, Error = 0.0; P < nPatterns; P++)
     {
       for (J = 0; J < nOutputNodes; J++)
       {
         float Temp = TargetOutput[P][J] - Out2[P][J];
         Error += Temp * Temp;
       }
     }

     // Average error over all patterns.
     Error /= nPatterns * nOutputNodes;

     // Print iteration number and error value.
     fprintf(stderr,"Iteration %5d/%-5d Error %f\r",
       Q, nIterations, Error);
     KeyboardRequest = 0;

     if (Q % ErrorFreq == 0)
       fprintf(ErrorFile, "%d %f\n", Q, Error);        // to file
     // Terminate when error satisfactory.
     if (Error < ErrorLevel)
       break;
   }
 }
 // End iterate loop.
```

```
// Display error, iterations, etc.
for (P = 0, Error = 0.0; P < nPatterns; P++)
{
  for (J = 0; J < nOutputNodes; J++)
  {
    float Temp = TargetOutput[P][J] - Out2[P][J];
    Error += Temp * Temp;
  }
}

// Average error over all patterns.
Error /= nPatterns *nOutputNodes;

// Print final iteration number and error value.
fprintf(stderr, "Iteration %5d/%-5d Error %f\n", Q,
        nIterations, Error); /* to screen */
fclose(ErrorFile);

// Print final weights.
if ((WeightsOutFile = fopen(szWeightsOut,"w")) == NULL)
{
  cout << " Can't write file\n" << Netname << szWeightsOut;
  exit(1);
}

for (H = 0;  H < nHiddenNodes; H++)
  for (I = 0;  I <= nInputNodes; I++)
    fprintf(WeightsOutFile, "%g%c", W1[H][I],
            I%ITEMS==ITEMS-1 ? '\n':' ');

for (J = 0;  J < nOutputNodes;  J++)
  for (H = 0;  H <= nHiddenNodes;  H++)
    fprintf(WeightsOutFile,  "%g%c", W2[J][H],
            J%ITEMS==ITEMS-1 ? '\n':' ');

fclose(WeightsOutFile);
```

```
  // Print final activation values.
  if ((ResultsFile = fopen(szResults,"w")) == NULL)
  {
    cout << " Can't write file \n" << Netname << szResults;
    ResultsFile = stderr;
  }

  // Print final output vector.
  for (P = 0; P < nPatterns; P++)
  {
    cout << ResultsFile << P;
    for (J = 0; J < nOutputNodes; J++)
      cout << ResultsFile << Out2[P][J];
    cout << ResultsFile << "\n" << PatternID[P];
  }
  fclose(ResultsFile);

// Free memory used for matrix.
    FreeMatrix(Out0, nPatterns);
    FreeMatrix(Out1, nPatterns);
    FreeMatrix(Delta1, nPatterns);
    FreeMatrix(Delw1, nHiddenNodes);
    FreeMatrix(W1, nHiddenNodes);
    FreeMatrix(Out2, nPatterns);
    FreeMatrix(Delta2, nPatterns);
    FreeMatrix(Delw2, nOutputNodes);
    FreeMatrix(W2, nOutputNodes);
    FreeMatrix(TargetOutput, nPatterns);
    free(PatternID);
  }
  fclose(RunFile);                    // Close run file.
}

// main program: creates and runs a back-propagation network

  void main(int argc, char *argv[]) {

    BackProp Bp;                      // instance of a back-prop
                                      // network
    char *Netname = *argv;            // Netname is read from
                                      // argument list.
```

```
   // Read arguments from DOS command line.
   for (; argc > 1; argc—)
   {
     char *arg = *++argv;
     if (*arg != '-')
       break;
     switch (*++arg)
     {
       case 'e':   sscanf(++arg,  "%d",  &Bp.ErrorFreq);   break;
       case 'd':   sscanf(++arg,  "%f",  &Bp.ErrorLevel);  break;
       default:    break;
     }
   }
   if (argc < 2)
   {
     fprintf(stderr, "Usage: %s {-en -df} runfilename\n",
       Netname);
     fprintf(stderr, " -en => report error every n iterations\n");
     fprintf(stderr, " -df => done if sum squared error < f\n");
     exit(1);
   }

   // Open run file for reading.
   if ((Bp.RunFile = fopen(*argv, "r")) == NULL)
   {
     cout << " Can't open file \n" << Netname << *argv;
     exit(1);
   }

   // Read first line from run file that contains number of runs
   // and other information for the network. Run file in this
   // example looks like this:
   // training.out training.err training.pat weight.wts } These
   // training.wts 100 100 9 4 2 0.15 0.075     } two lines are
   //                                           } on one line
   //                                           } in file.
   // Pattern, weight, and other input files consist of numbers
   // separated by spaces.
   fscanf(Bp.RunFile, "%d", &Bp.nRuns); // Scan for number of
                                        // runs.
   Bp.Iterate(*Netname);   // Iterate a back-prop network.
};
```

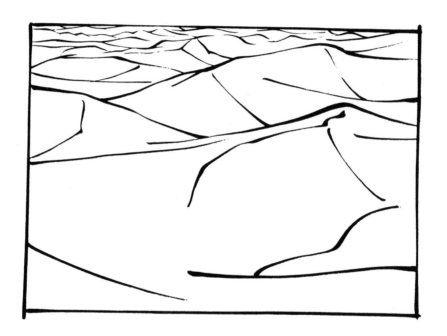

CHAPTER 7

Designing with Objects

When you have names and forms, know that they're provisional.

The Tao, like a well, is used but never used up.
— *Lao-tzu*

Any program when running is obsolete. If a program is useful, it will have to be changed. Any program will expand to fill all memory.
— *Utz's Law*

The Tao of objects is a process for designing programs that evolve in step with the world they model. Programs composed of objects are more powerful and flexible because of their built-in capacity for change. In this chapter, we'll reshape the object-oriented techniques we've discussed so far into a design philosophy.

Structured design suggests that you stop, think, and work out all the details before you start coding. Since most programmers use some form of structured design, you may expect an object-oriented design philosophy to be another complicated methodology requiring a long learning curve, excessive self-discipline, numerous diagrams and rules, and reams of documentation. It doesn't necessarily involve any of those, but it does require a fresh perspective.

Let's back up a little and briefly review structured design to see the kinds of problems software engineers must consider.

An Alternative to Chaos

Programmers often use guidelines to determine the best way to design a program. A methodology is a set of guidelines applied sequentially to generate a design from a set of specifications. Methodologies are popular because they give a step-by-step process for getting from the problem to the solution.

Structured programming was the first alternative to the lack of structure that led to chaos in large programming projects. This style emphasizes the structuring of programs into a pyramid shape like that found in the traditional business organizational chart. The bottom of the pyramid represents the blue-collar workers, the managers are at the top, and the middle contains the go-betweens who receive general commands from the managers and interpret them into specific commands for the workers.

A structured methodology generates a well-documented system in a model that's relatively easy to understand. It takes a system specification (a description of what the system should do) and generates a structured design. The methodology we'll examine here was pioneered by Yourdon, Constantine, and DeMarco and has been extended by Ward and Mellor to include real-time and data-driven systems.

You begin by describing the system (using the system specification, which was generated from the system analysis) with a series of data-flow diagrams. A DFD is a collection of bubbles and arrows. Each bubble represents a process or transformation that accepts data (incoming arrows) and produces a new type of data (outgoing arrows). Figure 7-1 shows a single bubble.

An entire system or a subset of a system can be represented by a single bubble. The process of arranging a system into a hierarchy of DFDs is called *leveling* (since the system is partitioned into levels of complexity). The DFD modeling process leads to a complete set of diagrams representing the system at various levels of complexity.

Bubbles let you view the system from different perspectives, from overview (a single diagram with one bubble and little detail) to fine detail (many diagrams, each with multiple bubbles).

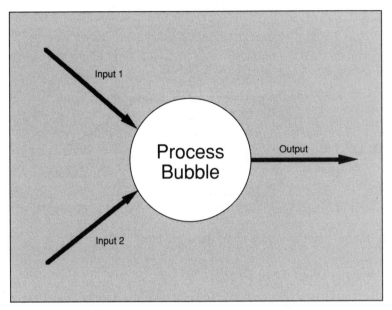

Figure 7-1. Each bubble in a DFD represents a process or transformation.

Once you've generated and checked the detailed DFDs, you generate a hierarchical structure chart from them (Figure 7-2). You can think of it as the business organization chart for the program.

The chart shows data moving in and out of boxes, which represent the transformations. It also shows which modules call which other modules. Combined with information about the data structures and transformations, the chart lets you code the program's components one at a time and independently of other components. Each box represents a function, and the data moving in and out of the box represents function arguments and return values.

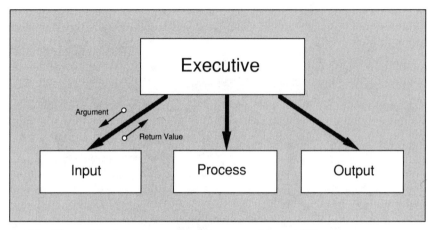

Figure 7-2. Hierarchical structure chart generated from DFDs.

What's Wrong With This Picture?

Structured techniques generate a much more maintainable design than anything produced with earlier techniques. So what's wrong with them? Easy — complexity, exhaustive design, and excessive documentation. But what can we do to improve them?

The high cost of software maintenance prompted the development of structured techniques, which are actually a way to generate good documentation for a system. Good documentation, of course, allows follow-up programmers to grasp what's going on, fix problems quickly, and expand the system. It also lowers maintenance costs, up to a point. The system's design may be clear but as restrictive as if the programmers had simply started coding.

How can we take a popular structured technique and apply it to object-oriented design? For example, a DFD assumes that data just flows around the system and passes through bubbles, where it's processed. DFDs stem from the perspective that all memory is a public resource. In this model, data elements are passive, raw materials that are acted upon by little processing plants (functional modules).

In an object-oriented design, messages move around the system, but "flow" isn't a particularly useful way of thinking about their movement. Objects keep their data to themselves and perform operations on their own data, eliminating the potential for the wrong functions acting on the right data and vice versa.

If you think of objects as little programs, the only useful place for DFDs is inside the object itself, and that's not very satisfying or helpful. DFDs are inappropriate for object-oriented design (ditto for structure charts) for one simple reason — they don't provide the kind of information you need. You should approach any object-oriented methodology that purports to use them with a healthy dose of skepticism.

(Beware of methodologies that use the input-processing-output scheme to develop the system model, as in "The input to the transmogrification phase is the annotated, fully redacted Framis Phase Model. The output is a Smith Perfection Chart showing all the completely specified objects and their interrelationships." This sort of thinking is part of the evolution from structured to object-oriented design. Expect to find it in early methodologies. When the first steam engine was installed on a boat, the designers attempted to take the rotary power from the steam engine and make it pull a set of oars, pick them up out of the water, move them forward, put them in the water, and so on. They didn't realize that a leap into a new methodology was necessary.)

In addition, the requirement (imposed by procedural languages) that all problems be massaged until they resemble computers leads to static designs and further problems. In other words, we try to make the problem conform to the computer and not vice versa. Although the implementation might be well-documented, a design change usually requires that we return to the beginning of the series of transformations that generated the design. Only at the beginning does the representation of the system map directly to the problem in the world.

In other words, the design isn't an accurate representation of the real-world system we're attempting to model. Instead, it represents the solution we build in the computer. Thus, it doesn't change easily when the real-world situation changes or our understanding of the problem changes.

Since a program inevitably changes, and since programmers (and managers) don't want to spend the time required to redocument those changes, the program's maintainers begin to encroach upon the original boundaries of the design. Eventually, these boundaries become fuzzy and the clarity of the design is lost — all because the design process requires too many transformations and too much documentation to support easy changes. In the words of guru Larry Fogg, "Too much magic causes software rot."

In most traditional organizations, change is an enemy or, at best, a mysterious entity to be avoided. Consider the plight of many traditional businesses faced with changing markets. In the past, changes could be slowly integrated into the company after months or years of consideration. Now, things are happening too quickly for every change to be propagated all the way to the top of the organization, learned by the CEO and the board of directors before it's implemented, and propagated back down.

Management consultants are proposing that individual workers be given the power and responsibility to make the adaptations that affect their work. Those who are directly affected by something should be able to experiment with it. They see the changes first, can see how a system should evolve, and are the first to notice the effects of any adaptations. They're in the best position to experiment. In theory, they make the best decisions.

Programmers, too, must be in a position to experiment for both creative and practical reasons. Object-oriented design encourages such experimentation.

If you're using structured design techniques now, you should continue to use them with object-oriented programming. Just remember that older structured design techniques don't support inheritance or formal reuse, whereas these notions are of primary concern when designing object-oriented systems. You must apply a bit of careful judgment and ad hoc techniques to solve these problems.

Real-time structured design methods (like Ward-Mellor) and entity-relationship diagrams are good starting points for object-oriented design. Object-oriented programming builds on structured programming; if you're using good structured techniques, you should build on what works but design with a bit more flexibility to accommodate reuse.

Programming for Change

Consider how you interact with the world. You begin by collecting the best information you can and creating a model of the world based on that information. (This happens, of course, at brainwave speed.) Then you behave based on that model.

The model is inevitably flawed, and every moment of your life you gain new experience and have new thoughts that modify your model of the world. You conceive multiple models to represent various aspects of the world. Many of these models are regularly updated (by new technology, new programming techniques, how you perceive a compiler's operation, the ways you communicate), while others may continue to work just fine for your purposes and don't need to be updated (the nocturnal activities of the African dung beetle, the latest improvements to BASIC). You constantly modify your models to adapt to new external and internal information.

As you use a model of the world, you almost always gain new information from it and change the model accordingly. In fact, if a model stops changing, chances are you aren't using it. In a sense, the model is a state indicator of the learning process.

Suppose you move to a new area and need to go to the grocery store. You get a map and study it until you discover a way to get there. On the way, you observe your surroundings and remember them, making a model in your head. The model encompasses only a portion of the area you live in, but if it gets you to the grocery store it's extremely functional. As you go new places, you expand your model of the area until you can get to many places without consulting a map.

Let's look at the same example using structured techniques, which require all the research up front. You would have to memorize the entire map before you went anywhere. What if the map changes or the streets don't correspond to the map? There isn't much allowance for change unless you redraw portions of the map and memorize it again. We don't know anyone who works this way, but programmers are expected to.

Suppose you wanted to take up photography. Books on photography are plentiful, and you could read indefinitely about how to take pictures, but at some point you'd need to get out and take some pictures yourself to relate to the text you're reading.

The model we create when we build a computer program is similar to the one we create when we represent something from the outside world within ourselves. The computer expression of the model is more concrete, is in a different medium, and takes longer to change, but it still expresses our current understanding of an external system. In the same way that we change our models of the world to adapt to new internal or external information, we want to change our computer models of the world to adapt to exactly the same kind of information. Why not behave as if design were a learning process?

Here are some object-oriented design guidelines:

1. You can't know everything about a system before you design it. Don't even try. Some things can only be learned when the system is running for the first time (or when it's been running for a week or a year).

2. Your goal should be to get something working as soon as possible and to use the model to gain further information about the problem.

   Your first model may be only vaguely like the external system (remember how you thought cars worked when you were in kindergarten?), but the ideas can be refined and modified as you learn. Object-oriented programming supports change, so use that to your advantage. It also prevents "overkill programming" — spending too much time creating a program to solve problems that will never arise.

Use creeping featurism, but add the features as they're requested to allow immediate feedback. Object-oriented programming tends to isolate the effects of one part of a system from another, so changing one part of a model usually doesn't affect other parts.

3. Plan on changing the design as you go. This doesn't mean "do something and throw it away," as previous techniques have suggested, but rather "start someplace reasonable and grow as you learn." The goal is not to create a static design, so assume from the start that the design will change.

4. It's OK to make mistakes, but try to make them as early in the process as you can.

    The best way to find out if you've made a mistake is to try out your design. Your mistake is probably isolated, so you won't throw the entire design away; instead, you'll just modify a section to reflect your new learning.

One of the old bugaboos of structured programming and design is management's desire to measure programmer productivity. Object-oriented programming and design increase productivity by providing libraries of objects that can be reused and by allowing the production of more generic, easier-to-maintain code.

Unfortunately, it's very hard to measure the effect object-oriented programming has on programmer productivity. Most of the standard metrics are based on measuring lines of code written. With object-oriented programming, we want to measure lines of code *not* written; that is, the amount of code reused across other applications. We don't have tools that do this today, but perhaps future browsers and inspectors will keep track of when we reuse code. For programmer productivity to really increase, reuse must be rewarded.

Object-Oriented System Design

It would be convenient — but, unfortunately, unrealistic — to expect programmers and users to have complete knowledge of the system. First, we can seldom delude ourselves into believing we know the system at any given time; second, the system we're designing and the techniques (the compilers, languages, and hardware) we're using are evolving. Most of us approximate and speculate at every turn.

On the less technical, more personal side, two convenient approximations are often made in software design projects: The designer completely understands the problem before beginning, and the user reads the manual and thus knows the program completely before using it.

Demanding perfection from users simply isn't practical. Many system designers acknowledge that users probably don't read the manual and may at first understand only a fraction of what the program is supposed to do. These enlightened designers make the system work for the user by anticipating that users will be diverse and evolving. The system must allow users to learn (modify their internal models) and to adapt the system when their problems change (adapt to external changes).

Object-oriented design offers a solution: You can design objects anytime, whenever the need moves you. Every system is assumed to be in flux; every program is assumed to be dynamic. You can create, modify, and delete new objects at run time without disrupting the system.

Say you're designing an editor. You began (sensibly enough) by creating a *file_editor* type. This type can open a file, read it into a buffer, move a cursor around in the buffer, find text, insert and delete text, and so on. As the type definition develops, so does the need to test it. You decide that the simplest way to do that is to make it aware of the screen. In other words, the type will show you on the screen what it's doing offscreen.

To be aware, the *file_editor* screen must have some knowledge of how text can be displayed. It needs to know where the display starts and ends and where the cursor should sit on the screen; in short, how to map the buffer to the screen. You add these features and everything works. Now you begin testing the *file_editor*'s features, one by one.

Two things happen. First, by using the system in a screen editor, you begin to see possibilities you hadn't before imagined. Since the text display can vary and be controlled, you realize that multiple pieces of text can exist on the screen at one time. Second, you now want to use the *file_editor* to display everything — multiple files, sections of text for prompting, help screens, even the line at the bottom of the editor that prompts for input for text searches and other activities. Thus, the *file_editor* type is undergoing a reuse test.

Does the type adapt itself easily to these new situations? After answering "no," you begin modifying the type to make it more general and soon run afoul of the complexity test.

With all the files, views, and cursors, one change can create many new problems. The *file_editor* type is failing the overambitious-object test: It tries to do too much and as a result can't be reused. A mature type, especially one that has evolved through several redesigns, often becomes too complex for further evolution. Take confusing complexity as a sign that an object has a design problem. It may not, but it's worth a look.

In this case, you discover a better design when reusing the *file_editor*. You should have created a *text_buffer* type that knows about big chunks of text, how to move around in the text, how to insert and delete, and so on. This type can be used for files, constant strings, standard input, and one-line user prompts with equal ease. You then derive from type *text_buffer* a *file_buffer* that knows how to read and write files (*write()* is a virtual function in *text_buffer*). Finally, a *text_viewer* type contains a *text_buffer*, either a plain one or a *file_buffer* (since virtual functions are used, it doesn't need to know the specifics).

A *text_viewer* knows all about views of the text — starting and ending points of the piece being displayed, the display cursor, and so on. It resolves the changes in a *text_buffer* with the way it appears onscreen. (It also isolates the changes necessary when going to a new platform or changing from text-mode to graphics-mode displays.)

The need to design, experiment, and create occurs every time you (the designer) interact with the system. It isn't isolated in any of the activities (object discovery, object assembly, system construction, system maintenance, and object reuse) because you're always learning new things about the internal and external factors and about design itself.

Only in the simplest cases will you understand the entire problem and get the design correct the first time. It's a koan: To design it you have to build it, but to build it you have to design it. In the end, the system grows, so it's important to germinate as soon as possible. Start building, and you'll start designing.

The Five Stages of Object Design

Let's look at a way to tackle object-oriented programming. I've used this approach successfully and have observed that programmers' attention is held during the design process because they can immediately apply the design or imagine how it will work in code. The design approach, like object-oriented programming itself, thrives on being as close as possible to the end result.

This technique assumes that type design is driven by system design (you can't develop good types in a vacuum), that a type doesn't spring fully formed and perfect from the hand of its creator, and that a type is only mature after it has been modified a few times to meet the creator's changing external needs and internal understanding.

Throughout this discussion, remember that the only goal is to define the objects. If you see a better approach to your problem, try it! What counts is coming up with a good set of objects. The test of your design will be how well it models the situation in the real world, not whether you followed the proper steps in producing it.

You may think it takes years of experience to design types properly and to know to put a particular function member or data in a type. To dispel this myth and prevent you from wasting too much time on early design decisions, let's look at this five-step technique for describing the creation and maturation of types.

1. **Object discovery**

   This is where you try to determine which object types will solve the problems your system presents. At this point, you're more concerned with the boundaries and gross interactions between objects than with the details. We'll take a closer look at this step shortly.

2. Object assembly

As you start building the objects, you'll discover you need data and function members to make the internals of the object work properly. You may also discover you need other objects, either as members of the type or to work in concert with some object in the system. A good way to uncover further type requirements during object assembly is to develop test programs for each type you create.

3. System construction

As you bring objects together in the final program, the system may require either new functionality in existing objects or entirely new objects.

4. System extension

In object-oriented programming, the dreaded system maintenance becomes just another step in the process. And it's not unpleasant — it's exciting because making a well-designed system more powerful is so easy. This is where you'll discover how well your system is designed. If it isn't as easy to extend as you'd like, expect to find weak points in your design. Once you find them, you can fix them.

Note that activities focus on object types, not systems. *Maintenance* means maintaining object types, the discrete subparts of your system. If your object types are "clean," building and modifying the system is simple.

5. Object reuse

When you build a new program using old object types, your new needs will stress the types' design. If the design doesn't easily fit into a new situation, here's where it will show up, and you'll see the parts that need to be changed.

At each stage, you get new information to guide you in type design. While it would be difficult and time-consuming to anticipate this information in a preemptive design, the information comes to you naturally as you pass through these stages. Although this philosophy of object-oriented design differs from past methodologies, implementing it is easy. In fact, many programmers tend to work this way regardless of the methodology they're supposed to be following.

More on Object Discovery

The first of the five stages merits a closer look. What criteria do you use to discover objects? Here are some guidelines:

- Look for external factors, those necessary for interactions between objects and the world outside the system. You may discover some data members and methods at this point, but you'll primarily be discovering the objects themselves.

- Look for boundaries in the real world. For example, the boundary between memory and disk is often reflected as a boundary in your system.

- Look for things that are duplicated in a system. In a keyboard, for instance, *button* is an obvious object. A car has four wheels and four doors; an air traffic control system deals with planes. If you add new types of planes to the air traffic control system, for example, it should still know how to handle them.

- Hunt for the least common denominator in a system (the smallest unit). If you're manipulating text, that could be a character, a word, a line, or a group of text with the same attributes, depending on how you intend to use the text.

- Think of new situations where you might use the type. Does it work? Does it adapt easily? Imagine, for example, a very large version of your system or your system in a new situation with new requirements or constraints.

- Separate the actions and characteristics that change from those that stay the same.

- List the data your system needs to know about. Look for data that seems to belong together. Collect these data elements into an object.

- Look for data you want to hide or protect from careless modification. Such things usually belong inside an object.

- Look for common interfaces between objects and put them in an abstract base type.

- Imagine the types you'd need to put the project together right now. Write *main*() as if you had those types to find out the kind of functionality they need.

- Look for initialization and cleanup activities. These should be performed inside constructors and destructors.

An Example

Consider a sophisticated management system that attempts to solve the problems inherent in setting up a video store. Most such stores are an exercise in frustration: You know the kinds of movies you want, but you usually don't know the titles you want.

By reading the box containing the video, you see what the movie distributor wants you to see ("This movie is *Star Wars*, *Lawrence of Arabia*, and *Gone With the Wind* all rolled into one. Every single reviewer loved it!"). You also get a three-paragraph description of the movie, written by someone who may or may not have actually viewed it and who was in any case bound to say positive things. You won't find really valuable information. For instance, if all the movie reviewers gave it a thumbs-down, no reviewers will be quoted on the box. It won't tell you whether all your neighbors hated it or the amount of humor, sex, or violence in the movie. These are things you can only find out by renting the movie.

Now imagine a video store that doesn't have shelves filled with movie cartons. Instead, you step up to a computer (or to a person operating a computer) and say: "Today I'm in the mood for a movie with a science-fiction theme that's set in the near future, that my favorite reviewers liked, and that has moderate levels of nudity and low levels of profanity and violence."

The machine then brings up the titles of movies you haven't seen before and that aren't currently checked out and puts them in order according to your personal profile. You can get more information about each title, such as the actors and directors, reviews, biographies of the people involved in making the movie, and even a graphical picture of the box (if you insist). If the movie was never released in theaters and thus was not reviewed, you can get other criteria, such as the results of a poll of people who have viewed the movie (including information about gender and age group). In short, you get the kind of information you really need to select a movie.

When you choose a movie, the clerk gets it from the back and uses a bar-code reader to enter the number into the computer, which generates a receipt and does all the necessary bookkeeping.

Part of this video-store management system is obviously an elaborate database system (which needs to be updated easily at regular intervals and from various sources, including the customers themselves). Part of it is the user interface, part is the bar-code interface, and part is the bookkeeping system.

The Object-Oriented Design System

Before discovering objects, you need to make lists of:

- Data (information the system needs to know or remember)
- Events (situations the system needs to respond to)
- Functionality (what the system needs to do)
- Obvious objects (anything that leaps out at you). For example, you may know from the beginning that you want to use a windowing interface.

Don't try to make these lists perfect or complete — the act of putting together the model (not creating a list) will ensure that the system is complete. The lists only act as ticklers to help you find the objects in your system. By looking at the lists, you'll see patterns that suggest objects. When you discover enough objects to describe the system without the lists, you'll throw the lists away.

For some systems, the data list will give you the most information and will be the easiest to compile. Other systems will be primarily event-driven (usually referred to as *real-time systems*); for others you may think more easily in terms of what you want it to do, so the functionality list will be the easiest.

Remember that it's OK to make mistakes or omissions — an object-oriented system makes it easy to modify the program when you discover inconsistencies with the real world. Because objects keep their data and functions to themselves, changes in the system tend to be localized rather than propagated throughout the system as in procedural languages.

When you compile the data list, feel free to group data items that are likely to form an object. For example, a *person* object will probably contain a name, address, age, sex, membership number, and list of movies the person has seen, so it makes sense to combine those items.

Events aren't always as obvious as data. A mouse, for instance, is actually an event generator. Every time you push a button or the mouse crosses some boundary, that's an event. We usually handle events by creating a representation of a state and changing that state based on the current state and the current event. We often refer to this as a *state machine*. The rest of the system makes decisions based on the current state.

For example, we can implement a context-sensitive help system with a state machine. Every time the user changes context (by making a selection from a menu, for example), the help state machine changes state. When the user asks for help, the type of help given depends on the state (the context). Looking at a collection of events will often help you discover an object.

(It's interesting to think of the current moment as an external factor while it's happening but as an internal factor as soon as it's past. It changes the state of the individual. We can think of the individual as a state machine that changes based on input from external factors.)

Keep in mind that this is an iterative process, an approach intended only to give you a framework and get you started. The framework may change as you sketch out the system, but in the end it's unimportant — the goal is to determine what your objects should be. As you fill in the details of your sketch, you'll discover new objects and new relationships between objects.

Let's begin by compiling the four lists for our video-store management system:

Data

Customer
    Name
    Address
    Customer ID
    List of movies previously checked out
    Preference list
Profile
    ?
Movie
    Name
    Quantity
    Price Structure
    Evaluation List
Rental Transaction
    Date
    Customer
    Movie list (What if not all of the movies are returned?)
Business report
    Date range
    Data list
    Data format
    Calculations

Events

Customer asks for range of movies.
Customer asks for further data on movie.
    Reviews
    Local opinion
    Box description/pictures

Personnel: actors, directors, and so on

Theater runs and receipts

Customer checks out movie(s).

Customer asks for computer-generated movie selection based on customer profile.

Customer asks for best-seller based on overall popularity.

Customer returns movies (possibly not all), possibly checks out more.

Customer gives opinion of movie.

New movies arrive.

New movie data arrives.

Old movies are discarded/replaced.

Manager requests report.

Functionality

Create new customer profile.

Create new movie profile.

Create movie request profile; combine with customer profile.

Search for appropriate movies.

Create management report.

Check out movie.

Check in movie.

Update profiles.

Obvious Objects

Windows

Database

Error handler

Time and date string

After putting these lists together, you need to begin discovering objects. By this time, you may already have seen some objects (in the data list, for instance, where a group of data — customer, movie, rental transaction, and business report — obviously belongs together).

Functionality may require more work. You may want to put it in a block chart as shown in Figure 7-3.

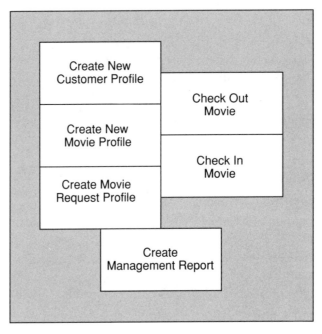

Figure 7-3. Block diagram.

Now take an individual section and begin analyzing it for objects. Think about what you want that section to produce. (Will the thing produced be an object? Will the producer be an object?) What do you want to be portable, or at least retargetable (user interface, other hardware, operating system interface)? Wrap these in an object.

Does the block diagram suggest any boundaries that reveal new objects? In a networking system, for example, the network itself is a boundary; you may need to create "transaction objects" to send across the network.

As you discover objects, consider what those objects need to know. Should they maintain this information themselves or get it from another object? Make a note of that object, even if it belongs in another section.

Notice in the functionality list the recurrence of the word *profile*. This may suggest an abstract concept called *profile* that you represent in an abstract base type. All profiles may then be derived from that type. This is just an early observation, however, and in the end may not be appropriate.

The Complexity Test

Make sure your objects don't become too complex. Just because you need a particular object, that object shouldn't necessarily be part of a single type rather than a type hierarchy or composition. Don't fall victim to "premature specification."

In an earlier example concerning the file-editing type, the type's complexity was revealed during code reuse. The type was very difficult to apply to a new situation because it was specific to a certain problem. The solution was to factor it into smaller, more discrete parts.

If you have a background in structured techniques, you may recognize the complexity test as equivalent to testing for low coupling and high cohesion. This is a little harder to judge with objects, since coupling and cohesion have been tests for functions. An object that does what you want always looks great; the test of goodness comes when you try to reuse it.

The complexity test is also important during object assembly, when you'll discover whether your objects are too complex. As you add and test functions, things may get out of hand. Adding new functions will be difficult because the type is managing so much by itself. This is an indication that the type needs to be factored into smaller sections and assembled through inheritance or composition.

Factoring results in several types, each of which is easier to implement because it's easier to think about. In addition, the objects will probably be easier to reuse.

OOP and GUI

One of the areas where object-oriented programming pays off most is in graphical user interfaces, such as Microsoft Windows, OS/2 Presentation Manager, and the Macintosh. This is partly due to the inherent complexity of programming for GUI systems.

This might seem paradoxical, considering how easy these systems are for application users. If you look under the hood of a GUI application, however, you'll find that everything that's easy for the user requires very hard work on the part of the programmer. Windows has an Applications Programming Interface of more than 500 functions that must be called to do things like create a window, select the font, invalidate areas of the screen, track the mouse, and so on. OS/2 Presentation Manager is several times this complex.

Object-oriented programming languages help hide the complexity of GUI programming by providing objects that encapsulate access to the API. After all, you probably want a window in your application that's just like the standard window type, but a little different. With an object-oriented language, you don't need to learn and make dozens of function calls to create a window. Instead, you just need to know about the predefined object types and then use inheritance to add new behaviors.

Another, more subtle reason for the link between GUI systems and object-oriented programming is that most graphical systems are message-based. For example, Windows and OS/2 treat user events (such as clicking the mouse or pressing a key) as messages sent to the application. In the OOP world, you can send these messages directly to the corresponding window object and handle it just like any other method in the system. This means less code is required to process user events in an object-oriented language.

Libraries and Frameworks

Part of the strength of object-oriented programming lies in the creation of libraries of reusable objects. We've already seen the beginnings of this with libraries such as Turbo Power's Object Professional library for Turbo Pascal, Zinc's Interface Library for C++, and others. These provide generic types for user-interface components such as windows, dialogs, and, in some cases, data management with linked lists and tables. I recommend these libraries both as a way to increase your productivity and as examples of good object-oriented programming techniques.

If you extend the notion of abstraction one step beyond such visual elements as windows and dialogs, you can conceive of generic applications themselves. A library that allows you to extend a generic application is known as an *application framework*. You can think of an application framework as a do-nothing application that can be extended to do almost anything. Although programming with an application framework may seem unfamiliar at first, it builds on many of the concepts presented here to give you an even higher level of productivity.

Skeptic's Corner

You may be saying to yourself: "This makes a lot of sense. It's pretty much the way I write programs anyway. But what about large projects? Will this technique still apply?"

Remember that object-oriented programming supports systems that change throughout their lifetime. The model focuses on the process rather than the goal. Your objective, then, should not be to build a system but to "grow" a system. The most elaborate garden must be planted; the objects in the garden grow at their own rates. At each stage of development, the garden has an effect. It may not be mature, but it's functional.

It's also real — something people can look at, work with, and improve. You can see how things work now and imagine a direction to move in the context of the current system. If some plants aren't effective in the garden, you pull them out and plant something else. Eventually, with time and continuous design, the garden matures into a phase in which change consists of only minor adjustments.

You could design a garden as a finished system and use fully mature plants that look exactly the way you want them. This approach is very expensive initially and very expensive to change. The fact that you have good plans (good documentation) helps you understand the vision of the original designer, but it doesn't take into consideration that the requirements of the world may change or that you may understand something the original designer didn't. You'll still have to develop new plans for a major change and tear out some expensive plants. Even minor changes (those that don't involve design changes) are expensive because a system like this isn't designed to be modified; it's designed with the assumption that it's finished.

Object-oriented programming lets you start with a small garden and eventually increase the acreage, start with a large garden of immature plants (some of which may be changed as the garden matures), or start with older, existing plants and add young, new ones. Not only can you build programs more quickly, the programs can be adapted to the new knowledge and new situations that have been the nemesis of old-style programming techniques.

The Art of Software Design

All this makes object-oriented design sound a lot like art, which isn't a bad analogy. Creating software, like art, requires interpretation on the part of the artists; calling it "engineering" may be one of the more creative misapplications of that word. Getting a group of artists to work together is a difficult process; they focus on the product, not the company. There's no physical structure (like a manufacturing plant) in a software group to hold it together once the project is complete.

Can object-oriented programming techniques change this? Probably. One person can manage much larger, more complex bodies of code. Reuse of libraries of existing code is supported. The compiler controls the integration of a project, so you don't rely on tests that may or may not be created and administered. Objects are little programs, so each person can have the satisfaction of creating a complete work, even if it is later integrated into a larger one. All this helps teams create and work together and improves accountability, localization of bugs and changes, learning in a large project, and flexibility.

Structured techniques came about because existing languages couldn't support large projects — things broke down when the projects got too big, and a great deal of planning was necessary to prevent this breakdown. Using an object-oriented language that supports large projects, you can plan a lot less, code sooner, and test the real thing (or something close to it) instead of trying to imagine whether or not it's what you want.

During object assembly, consider the initialization and cleanup of each object. Should these activities be part of object discovery and CASE support? Almost certainly.

You're "growing" your objects from the time you start thinking about them. Writing them is the rapid phase of growth, but growth nonetheless: You start with the type framework, then add and test functions and function bodies. During system construction and extension, you may add more to the type.

Object design occurs in all five stages: object discovery, object assembly, system construction, system extension (not maintenance), and object reuse; that is, throughout the lifetime of a system. We've only pretended we could force design to occur in the first phases of a project, and not later, thinking this would make it less expensive to maintain. Good documentation helps, but things still change and new designs are still required. A rigid design, no matter how well it's documented, eventually loses its internal structure in the face of these changes.

And that's it for this introductory study of object-oriented techniques. I hope you can see that the sophisticated techniques in object-oriented programming languages help programmers create more productive, creative, flexible programs designed to evolve with the real-world problems they model. Object-oriented programming is both a method and a philosophy, one that can dramatically narrow the gap between the real world and the world of the computer.

From here on, try to construct your programs out of objects, and check out the reference list (Appendix B) if you want to delve further into this fascinating methodology.

Afterword

Never make predictions, especially about the future.
— Samuel Goldwyn

Samuel Goldwyn may not be an Eastern philosopher, but his words ring true. Despite his advice, I'm going to look ahead at the future of object-oriented programming. But first, you may be wondering how this afterword came about.

About two and a half years ago, I spoke with Gary about doing an article on object-oriented programming for the now-legendary *Micro Cornucopia*. Strangely enough, I also met Bruce Eckel through the pages of that magazine. His article on C++ appeared a few pages after mine, so it's fitting that the three of us meet again in print in Gary's book on the philosophy and practice of object-oriented programming.

I recently had the pleasure of working with Bruce on Borland's OOP World Tour, where we taught object-oriented programming in C++ and Turbo Pascal around the world. At our final destination, Tokyo, the two of us took a train out to the old capital, Kamakura, and explored the variety of temples there. As we walked through the exquisite gardens, amidst the statues and trees, Bruce told me about Gary's book on the Tao of objects. It sounded like a fascinating way to learn about object-oriented programming. After all, programming is part art, part science, and certainly part philosophy. One of the areas we talked about was the future of object-oriented programming.

The philosophical side of object-oriented programming may well endure beyond structured programming and design as well as other programming approaches. But as you continue down the path of object-oriented programming seeking your own enlightenment, it's sometimes reassuring to know that the art and science are maturing. For this reason, I was asked to look further down the path to see what's in store for object-oriented programmers. Along the way I'll discuss the evolution of hardware and software, the impact on OOP, tools beyond OOP, and some of the myths of object-oriented programming.

The Evolution of Hardware and Software

One of the obvious trends that affects object-oriented programming is the changing hardware. As I look across my desk to the "computer museum" in the corner of my office, I can see the progress hardware has made in the past decade. We've gone from 64K Z80 CP/M machines like the Osborne I that ran Ron Cain's Small-C and Turbo Pascal 1.0 (and had room to spare!) to my new four-megabyte 386SX that runs Turbo C++ and Turbo Pascal 6.0. And I'm not at all surprised by the fact that the Osborne cost more than the 386. Certainly we'll see the same level of improvements in hardware in the next decade. My 386, barely a month old, is already considered old hat by the hardware aficionados touting the latest 486s. Let them laugh; I'll catch up with the 586 or perhaps even the 686.

So what impact does this have on our software? Utz's law, as Gary stated in Chapter 7, tells us that "any program will expand to fill all memory." My current crop of C++ and Turbo Pascal tools doesn't exhaust all my RAM, but by the time I load a few TSRs and Windows 3.0 the ceiling is definitely in sight.

Utz must have been thinking about graphical environments when he coined his law. Much of the hardware horsepower we have achieved in the last 10 years has gone toward making powerful, easy-to-use environments like Windows. These environments make computing what it should be: easy, powerful, and fun.

But as any programmer knows, the easier you make things for the user, the harder they are for the developer. Programming for today's graphical environments is exceedingly difficult using traditional tools. So if Windows is the future, how do programmers get there? The answer is, of course, by using object-oriented programming.

If you look at the development tools used in graphical environments, you'll see that an overwhelming majority are object-oriented. Certainly DOS programmers benefit from OOP, but in graphical environments it has become a necessity.

In some sense, the rapidly expanding hardware field has forced us down the path of object-oriented programming. And although there's a learning curve to adopting OOP, it's one that's worth overcoming.

The more you use OOP, the more excited you'll become. As one programmer put it, "When I program in OOP, I'm limited only by my imagination." Many programmers find that walls of complexity prevent them from building certain kinds of applications. With OOP, these barriers come tumbling down, slowly at first, then in an avalanche as you learn to create self-contained objects that tackle small problems for you. Your job is to piece these objects together into larger programs that take us into new application areas. After all, we've got to do something with the extra cycles on the 686.

OOP Horizons

Object-oriented technology will continue to improve over the next decade. Already the current crop of OOP tools from Borland, Zortech, The Whitewater Group, and others are in their second or later versions with major enhancements over earlier ones. Efforts toward standardization with groups such as ANSI and the Object Management Group, combined with the competitiveness of the marketplace, will ensure continued improvement in the languages. This means faster compilation, better run-time performance, and better tools for browsing, inspecting, and debugging.

I also expect that we'll continue to have a wide spectrum of OOP languages. The hybrid languages will coexist with pure OOP languages for years to come. And, as has happened in the past, newer languages will build on the OOP concepts that exist today to create the next generation of programming languages.

However, more important than improvements in the compilers or languages themselves are the enhancements to object libraries. Libraries and frameworks are the major leverage point in object-oriented programming because you don't have to reinvent the wheel every time you program. Instead, you can inherit automatically from libraries included with your compiler or from third-party sources.

Most of the libraries out there today are foundation libraries. That is, they supply generic components such as windows, dialogs, and data-management objects. While these are important building blocks, I believe that in the next decade we'll see the emergence of an object-oriented components industry.

This industry will be a combination of today's hardware components market, where generic, off-the-shelf components compete primarily in price and performance, and the commercial library market, where packages compete based on compatibility and functionality. Ideally, generic software objects will be mass-produced so that linked-list managers, windowing systems, file managers, and so on will be so widely available that no one will ever need to write these things again. Only then can a higher-level components industry emerge to supply specialized objects for vertical market applications.

Like the application-specific integrated circuit market, these components will be more expensive, but they'll provide a competitive advantage to buyers. At that point, the software market will belong not to the "wizards" who write every piece of software from scratch but to those who can work at higher levels, solving application problems by combining existing components.

Organizations will create libraries of objects that embody the operations of their business. One can imagine an investment bank creating objects to evaluate the investment potential of startup firms. These objects might have behaviors based on the knowledge acquired from specialized neural networks or heuristics based on the work of experts. Or an insurance company might develop a library of objects for transaction processing and risk assessment. No doubt some organizations will closely guard the libraries of objects they develop, considering them to be trade secrets as important as the formula for Coca-Cola. Other companies, in an attempt to recoup the large software development costs, will sell or license the libraries on the open market.

The ever-increasing cost of software development has made the library market a necessary part of our industry's economic survival. Object-oriented programming may well be the catalyst that allows us to move beyond our cottage-industry approach to an industrial revolution of software development.

Beyond Programming

Today, the most accepted way of developing software, even if you're using an object-oriented language, is primitive: You write code in a text editor, compile it, and test it. Yet we have created amazingly innovative, visual ways for our users to design machines, draw graphs, generate reports, assemble documents, and lay out newsletters. I suspect that once we've developed a sufficiently large base of object libraries, we'll need to develop higher-level tools for software development.

Already some systems, like Asymetrix's Toolbook and the NeXTStep environment on the NeXT machine, show how we can build applications visually. These systems are limited in the range of things that can be done without programming, but they fit well with the philosophy of object-oriented programming. The goal, after all, is to reduce the software development effort.

Similarly, many programmers in the mainframe world use CASE diagramming tools to analyze and validate their designs before writing a single line of code. Some of the integrated CASE systems enable automatic code generation, though maintenance of this code is usually difficult.

For many types of software development, a visual approach with the right object-oriented methodology could help eliminate even more of the traditional programming bottleneck. When we have objects as sophisticated as the applications themselves, we shouldn't have to write reams of code to combine them into complete systems.

I'm not saying that programming will disappear; on the contrary, evidence supports the belief that programming is a growing market. The growth of programmable products (spreadsheets, databases, even word processors) and the booming market for low-end programming tools attest to this. And someone will need to program these higher-level development systems as well as create libraries of objects for visual programming.

Challenges

We will face many challenges before reaching the stage of having huge object libraries and visual tools. One of these is widespread dissemination of OOP, which requires that the skills of legions of programmers be updated. The development of easy-to-use OOP languages should make this much easier. However, I often wonder how we will ever hope to integrate object-oriented programming concepts into older languages like BASIC, COBOL, and RPG. For individual programmers, having OOP skills will be an advantage for several years. Beyond that, it will become a requirement.

One of the toughest challenges lies in creating standards for object-oriented libraries. Today, most object-oriented languages support a mechanism for persistence that enables us to store and retrieve objects to and from disk. This lets us convert object data between languages, but we must take it a step further: We must be able to use object libraries from different languages in a given programming project with full access to all functionality.

Today, it's impossible to access objects written in C++ from Turbo Pascal or vice versa. In fact, you can't access objects directly between any two object-oriented languages without some kind of conversion and loss of functionality. This barrier must be overcome before interoperability between development systems can be achieved. There's no one perfect programming language, object-oriented or otherwise, and we need to be able to select the best language for the job independent of the class libraries. Otherwise, we'll either waste our efforts converting libraries between languages or lock ourselves into single-language solutions for all applications and cripple our productivity.

The Object Management Group is working to achieve common standards between languages. However, at some stage, object management support must be present in the operating system, where it belongs, so that all languages can use a common service.

Myths of OOP

If you've discussed object-oriented programming with other programmers, you've no doubt heard some of the myths. Where they are accepted, they hinder our progress in advancing object-oriented programming.

One myth says that object-oriented programming is a single language. But remember that OOP is a philosophy, an approach that can be done in many different languages. Don't confuse the limitations of any particular language or compiler with those of OOP itself.

Another myth is that object-oriented programming is inefficient. This is something I've heard programmers use to dismiss OOP without any investigation. Object-oriented programming with hybrid languages like C++ and Turbo Pascal proves that nothing is inherently inefficient in OOP; even the performance of older languages like Smalltalk has improved dramatically in recent years.

You may hear traditional DOS and mainframe programmers claim that OOP is only for graphics applications. However, OOP concepts are general-purpose and apply to all programs, graphical or not.

Yet another myth says that object-oriented programming is incompatible with existing languages and libraries. Of course, one of the advantages of using a hybrid language like C++ or Turbo Pascal is that you have complete and easy access to all your existing libraries. Even the pure object-oriented languages like Actor let you access external libraries written in C.

The final myth of object-oriented programming is that it's just old wine in a new bottle. Perhaps, once you get past terms like *method*, *message*, *polymorphism*, and *inheritance*, nothing is going on that can't be done in a traditional structured programming language. It *is* unfortunate that there are so many new terms, but make no mistake — the terms are different. A message is not the same as a function call, and inheritance is not the same as copying and pasting code.

Certainly one can mimic object-oriented programming in procedural languages (after all, that's how the earliest C++ compilers worked — by translating object-oriented code into standard C code), but the difference is one of practicality. Object-oriented programming languages provide built-in mechanisms that support encapsulation, inheritance, and polymorphism so that you can spend your time solving application problems rather than fighting with language compilers.

Going Down the Road

As you know, learning object-oriented programming is not a trivial task. Its concepts are easy — deceptively so. Applying the concepts is more difficult. To learn OOP, you must immerse yourself in objects, at least during the initial stages. Examine good OOP applications that come with your tools or are available on BBSs. And take to heart the examples Gary has presented in these pages. Build on the ideas presented here to create object-oriented games, simulations, expert systems, and business applications.

The most important piece of advice anyone can give you is to learn OOP by experimenting — first with other programmers' code or design and then with your own. If you keep your objects simple, you'll be amazed at how you can solve problems of exponentially increasing complexity with only a linear increase in effort. The key is to create objects that solve small pieces of the problem and reuse them. Then you can write your own future of object-oriented programming.

Zack Urlocker
December 1990

Glossary

abstract type   A specific kind of base type designed to be used strictly as a basis for other types. It has no instances and thus can only be used to derive new types. It specifies an interface for all types derived from it. You use an abstract type to group common code. For example, if you have several collection types, they may all inherit from a single abstract type. Also known as a *formal class* in some languages.

access specifier   A keyword that controls access to data members and methods within user-defined types. C++ has three: *private*, *protected*, and *public*. *Friend* can give access to external functions. Turbo Pascal has one, *private*. (See the individual definitions for *private*, *protected*, *public*, and *friend*.)

Actor   An object-oriented language for Microsoft Windows.

ancestor   The type from which a descendant type inherits characteristics and behaviors. Also known as a *base type*.

base type   Defines a common interface to a group of descendant types. It generalizes the intended uses for a hierarchy of types. In other words, it describes the range of messages an object of a type can handle.

behavior   Another name for a method declared within a type.

binding (early)   Resolving a method call at compile time.

binding (late)   Resolving a method call at run time. When we resolve a method call, we insert the code to determine the address (or another reference) of the method definition at the point where the method is called.

browser   A software tool for inspecting object hierarchies.

built-in type   A type (such as *double* or *char*) included in a language. The compiler already knows how to handle it and doesn't have to learn about it each time it encounters an instance of one.

chaos   Stochastic (or random) behavior occurring in a deterministic system.

characteristic   Another name for data declared within a type.

class   A user-defined type in C++.

composition   Including user-defined object types as parts of other object types, as opposed to derivation (inheritance).

constructor   A special kind of method that initializes a type. In C++, a constructor has the same name as its class:

```
class Flower {
public:
  Flower();      // constructor
};
```

In C++, the compiler calls a constructor by default whenever you define an instance of a class. The constructor will be called at the point of definition or during dynamic allocation when you use the *new* operator. A user-defined type (class) can have more than one constructor, but none of them can be virtual.

In Turbo Pascal, a constructor can have any legal name not already in use, though the identifier *Init* is often used:

```
Flower = object
  constructor Init;     { constructor }
end;
```

In Turbo Pascal, you must explicitly define and call (send a message to) a constructor. A user-defined type can have any number of constructors, but they can't be virtual because the virtual-method mechanism depends on the constructor to set up the link to the Virtual Method Table.

data hiding   Removing some data from public view. Also known as *data abstraction*.

data members   Characteristics of a type.

declaration   A declaration introduces one or more names (object, function, set of functions, type, method, template, value, or label) into a program without specifying the body (the implementation) of methods. A declaration tells the compiler that data or functions exist but not where or how they're used.

For example, the following are declarations in C++:

```
extern int x;
struct s;
class a;
```

These are definitions:

```
int a;
extern const c = 0;
struct s { int x; int y );
int behavior(int x) { return x + a; }
```

The following are Turbo Pascal declarations:

```
PointPtr = ^Point;
Location = object
  Fields;
  Methods;
end;
```

An example of a Turbo Pascal definition is:

```
A : integer;
```

When we declare a variable, we tell the compiler that space exists somewhere for the variable but not how it's implemented. We can declare a variable more than once, but we can only define it once.

definition   A function definition looks like a declaration except that it has a body. A body is a collection of statements enclosed in braces ({ }). Braces indicate the beginning and end of a block of code. In C++:

```
int behavior(int sex, int age)
{ /* Code here */ }
```

When we define a variable, we create space for it:

```
int X;
```

In Turbo Pascal:

```
procedure behavior;
  begin
    { code }
  end;
```

delete   A C++ operator that destroys a dynamic instance of an object type. It calls the destructor, then releases the memory allocated for the instance.

derivation   Another name for inheritance.

descendant   A type that inherits the characteristics and behaviors of another type. Also known as a *derived type*.

destructor   A special type of method that performs cleanup for a user-defined object type. In C++, a destructor has the same name as the class in which it's declared, preceded by a tilde:

```
class Insect {
public:
  Insect();            // constructor
  ~Insect();           // destructor
};
```

In Turbo Pascal, a destructor can have any legal name not already in use:

```
Insect = object
  constructor Create;   { constructor }
  destructor Remove;    { destructor }
end;
```

In Turbo Pascal, destructors can be static or virtual, and a type can have more than one destructor. A destructor can be inherited just like other methods.

In C++, all destructors in an inheritance hierarchy are called, not inherited. Thus, each object type that's dynamic must have its own destructor. Memory for static and automatic objects (instances of classes) is allocated and deallocated automatically by the compiler. Memory allocated for dynamic objects using the new operator, however, must be deallocated using the *delete* operator.

dispose   Turbo Pascal procedure for deallocating objects allocated on the heap:

```
Dispose(CirclePointer);
```

Alternatively (and preferably), you can call the destructor inside the *Dispose* call using the following extended syntax to clean up an object:

```
PtrMyObject = ^MyObject;
MyObject = object
  constructor Init;
  destructor Done;
end;
var
  P : PtrMyObject;
Dispose(P, Done);        { Call the destructor to }
                         { clean up properly. }
```

dynamic binding Another name for late binding. See *binding (late)*.

dynamic variable allocation A variable allocated on the heap and manipulated with pointers. Creating and destroying variables at run time instead of compile time. See *binding (late)*.

Eiffel A completely object-oriented language available on UNIX.

encapsulation Combining data (characteristics) with the methods (behaviors) for manipulating it; organizing code into user-defined types.

event An occurrence that affects a program from the outside world. Examples are keystrokes, mouse-button clicks, a character from a serial port, and occurrences triggered by the system (DOS, BIOS), such as a timer tick.

expert system Through a knowledge base of expert information, maps the input characteristics and behaviors of a system, problem, pattern, or object to a specific output system, problem, pattern, or object. Input characteristics can represent colors, sizes, processes, events, symptoms, and so on. Output represents a solution, advice, pattern match, decision, and so on.

friend   In C++, a function or method given permission to access a type (class) member. A friend can be a function or a class:

```
class SomeInfo {
int X;
public:
  friend void AFriend_function(X*, int);
                              // a friend function
  friend class AFriendClass;  // a friend class
};
```

hierarchy   A group of types derived from a base type.

hybrid language   Incorporates features of both imperative and object-oriented languages.

implementation   Describes how a user-defined type works; the interface describes how a type works. You can compile, but not link, code with just the interface description. Therefore, you can create different implementations later and link them in without recompiling the rest of the project. By separating the interface from the implementation, we isolate bugs and make experimentation easier.

inheritance   Organizing user-defined types into hierarchies.

initialization   Setting a variable or instance of a type to a specific value.

inspector   A tool for examining the data and methods of an object.

instance   A variable of a type. Also known as an *object*.

interface   In C++, the class declaration; in Turbo Pascal, the object definition. The interface says "here's what a type looks like, and here are its behaviors," but it doesn't specify how the type behaves; that's left to the implementation. The interface describes what a type does, while the implementation describes how the type works.

member functions In C++, another name for *methods*. Throughout this book we use *methods* as the generic term for the behaviors declared within a type.

message The name of a method passed to an instance of an object type. When you send a message to an instance of an object, you call one of its methods. To send a message to an instance of an object, you specify the object and the method you want to invoke. For example, if *AType* is an instance of an object and *Init* is a method, the following sends an *Init* message to the object. In C++:

```
AType.Init();
```

In Turbo Pascal:

```
AType.Init;
```

method In C++, a function declared within a class and used to access the data within the class. Also called a *member function*. In Turbo Pascal, a procedure or function declared within an object and used to access the data within the object.

model A mathematical representation of some aspect of the world.

neural network A neural network maps input to output in a similar manner to an expert system (see *expert system*), with one exception: It uses examples instead of rules to produce its output. Expert systems require complete information; neural networks can produce results from incomplete information. A neural network is therefore considerably more powerful than an expert system. It can solve problems where *if/then* rules are either unknown or difficult to compile, classify new problems using fuzzy logic, and predict (infer) new results from previous trends or patterns.

new   An operator (in C++) or procedure (in Turbo Pascal) for allocating space for a type on the heap and initializing the object in one operation. In C++, *new* is invoked with a constructor call:

```
Circle *ACircle = new Circle(30,30,30);
```

In Turbo Pascal, *new* is invoked with two parameters, a pointer name and a constructor call:

```
new(ArcPointer,Init(35,24,35));
```

object   In C++, an instance of a class (an object type). In Turbo Pascal, an instance of an object type; a record (data and methods) that can inherit.

Objective-C   An object-oriented language that combines C and Smalltalk.

override   Reimplement, redefine. Used to describe the reimplementation of methods by object types.

pointer   Contains the address of a variable. In C++, designated by "*":

```
int *intPointer;
```

In Turbo Pascal, the pointer is designated by "^":

```
IntPointer : ^Integer;
```

polymorphic type   A type that's not known until run time.

polymorphism   Single interface, many implementations. Specifically, calling a virtual method for a variable whose precise type isn't known at compile time. The behavior is established at run time via late binding.

private   In C++, any members following *private* can only be accessed by methods declared within the same class. In Turbo Pascal, any members following *private* can only be accessed by functions within the same unit.

protected In C++, any members following *protected* can only be accessed by member functions within the same class or by member functions of classes derived from this class.

public In C++, means "anyone can use it." Any members (methods or data) following *public* can be accessed without restriction. In Turbo Pascal, all methods are considered public unless *private* is used.

scope The lifetime and accessibility of a variable. Defines which parts of a program can access specific variables. For example, a variable declared within a function is local by default and can only be accessed by code within the function.

Smalltalk One of the earliest object-oriented languages. Developed by Xerox Palo Alto Research Center in the 1970s.

static instance An instance of an object type named in the *var* declaration (in Turbo Pascal) and allocated in the data segment and on the stack. In C++, static instances have global lifetimes and are initialized before *main( )* and cleaned up after *main( )*.

static method A method resolved by the compiler at compile time. See *early binding*.

strange attractor In phase space, an attractor is a point or limit cycle in a dynamic system that draws or attracts a system. In other words, as the system changes state, it can reach equilibrium (settle down) to a point or a cycle. A strange attractor is one that's broken up or fragmented in phase space. It represents a system whose order, when plotted in a time series, isn't obvious but shows itself in a shape (an order) in phase space.

**strong vs. weak
type checking**   A strong type-checking system accepts only those expressions that it can guarantee to be correct. A weak type-checking system will allow potentially unsafe expressions to pass through the compiler.

**structured
programming**   Combines two ideas: structured program flow (in other words, the flow of control of a program is determined by the syntax of the program code) and invariants (assertions that hold every time control reaches them).

type   The type of a variable tells us the range of values (or states) it can assume and the operators we can apply to it. Type is everything we can know about a class of objects that a variable or instance can represent.

type extensibility   The ability to add functionality to code. You derive new types (through inheritance) and add or modify behaviors and characteristics to suit your needs.

unit   In Turbo Pascal, a collection of constants, data types, variables, procedures, and functions that are compiled separately. If data members in a type are declared after the keyword *private*, any function, method, or procedure within a unit can access them but nothing outside the unit can.

user-defined type   A single structure containing the characteristics and behaviors for the type. In C++, we call a user-defined type a *class*; in Turbo Pascal, we call it an *object*. The compiler treats it like a built-in type. Throughout this book, we use *user-defined type* and *object type* interchangeably.

virtual method
A method resolved by the compiler at run time. See *late binding*. In C++, you declare a virtual method by preceding the method name with the keyword *virtual*:

```
virtual void Show();
```

In Turbo Pascal, you declare a virtual method by adding the keyword *virtual* after the method:

```
procedure Show; virtual;
```

Virtual Method Table
In Turbo Pascal, each type (object) has a VMT that contains information about the type, including its size and a pointer to the code implementing each of its virtual methods. When an instance of a type sends a message to a constructor, the constructor establishes a link to the VMT automatically.

Each type has one VMT; each instance of a type links to the type VMT. (Caution: Don't send a message to a virtual method before calling its constructor!) Turbo Pascal allows you to use the *{$R+}* switch to check for the proper construction of an instance of a type sending a message to an object type. If the instance hasn't been properly initialized (via a constructor), a range-check error occurs.

The C++ equivalent of the VMT is called a *VTABLE*. The pointer that points to the VTABLE is called the *VPTR*.

with
Turbo Pascal keyword. You can access a type's data members by using a dot (for example, *AType.Member*) or a *with* statement:

```
with AType do
begin
  X:= 2;
  Y:= 3;
  Z:= 4;
end;
```

References and Resources

If you want more information about C++, Turbo Pascal, modeling, chaos theory, or neural networks, the following books are worth looking into. They're only a sampling of the many works available on these subjects, but they reflect what I have on my shelves. Most of them have in some way contributed to my understanding of these tough topics.

In addition, a number of computer-related journals publish excellent articles on object-oriented programming (usually C++ and Turbo Pascal) in most issues: *AI Expert*, *C Gazette*, *Computer Language*, *C++ Report*, *Dr. Dobb's Journal*, *Journal of Object-Oriented Programming*, *Midnight Engineering*, *Programmer's Journal*, and *PC Techniques*. I recommend all of these for up-to-date information on techniques and the latest happenings in object-oriented programming.

Abraham, Ralph, and Christopher Shaw. *Dynamics: The Geometry of Behavior* **(four volumes). Santa Cruz, Calif.: Aerial Press, 1984-1989.**

A great introduction to and study of dynamics using pictures. If you really want to get a feel for chaos theory, look into this one. Starts with periodic behavior and works toward the harder stuff: chaotic and bifurcation behavior. Great personalized drawings.

Casti, John L. *Alternate Realities: Mathematical Models of Nature and Man.* **New York, N.Y.: John Wiley & Sons, 1989.**

A thorough mathematical discussion of modeling. Chapters on formal representation, cellular automata, catastrophe theory, chaos, and the relationship of modeling to the way we view the world.

Eberhart, Russel, and Roy Dobbins. *Neural Network PC Tools: A Practical Guide*. San Diego, Calif.: Academic Press, 1990.

A good, practical starting point for learning how to code a back-propagation neural network. Russ and Roy show you how to implement a neural network in C (code included) and present several excellent neural network case studies. Also discusses neural network implementation on a transputer-based hardware system.

Eckel, Bruce. *Using C++*. Berkeley, Calif.: Osborne/McGraw-Hill, 1989.

Not surprisingly, my favorite book on C++ programming; 600 pages of code, descriptions, and ideas about C++. It precedes the Turbo C++ compiler, so examples are developed around Zortech's C++ compiler but are easily adaptable to Turbo C++. Goes into some advanced topics I haven't covered: operator overloading, multiple inheritance, references, debugging, passing objects in and out of functions, and so on. A good book to explore and study if you want to get to the heart of C++.

Ellis, Margaret, and Bjarne Stroustrup. *The Annotated C++ Reference Manual*. AT&T, 1990.

This is currently the last word on C++ terminology and language description. If you want to know exactly how Bjarne defines C++, get a copy. Not for the faint-hearted, though, and certainly not light reading — as the title says, it's really a reference.

Gleick, James. *Chaos: Making a New Science*. New York, N.Y.: Viking Press, 1987.

The already classic introduction to chaos theory. Very easy, fun reading. Focuses as much on the people who rediscovered chaos as on the theory itself. Anyone interested in chaos should start here.

Hofstadter, Douglas, and Daniel Dennett. *The Mind's I*. New York, N.Y.: Bantam Books, 1981.

Like all of Hofstadter's books, this one really gets you thinking. A collection of stories and essays about self-reflection, self-consciousness, recursion, machines with souls, scientific speculation, and other mind-stretching ideas.

238

Meyer, Bertrand. *Object-oriented Software Construction.* **Englewood Cliffs, N.J.: Prentice-Hall, 1988.**

A good discussion of the issues and principles of software design using object-oriented techniques. Outlines the path leading to object orientation and generally aims to convince the reader to program with objects. The second half of the book (unfortunately for C++ and Turbo Pascal programmers) focuses entirely on Meyer's language, Eiffel, making it less useful than it could have been. Worth a look, though.

Mitchell, Stephen. *Tao Te Ching.* **New York, N.Y.: Harper & Row, 1988.**

This is the translation of Lao-tzu's wise book that I used to write this book. Highly recommended. "The master observes the world, but trusts his inner vision. He allows things to come and go. His heart is open as the sky."

***Object Professional User's Manual.* Scotts Valley, Calif.: Turbo Power Software, 1990.**

These three volumes of object-oriented, Turbo Pascal-style discussion accompany the fine Turbo Power object library for Turbo Pascal 5.5 and later. Complete source code for the library is included, so this package makes an excellent in-depth resource for ideas about object-oriented programming. Turbo Pascal programmers, in particular, should check out this library.

O'Brien, Tim. *Turbo Pascal, The Complete Reference.* **Berkeley, Calif.: Borland-Osborne/McGraw-Hill, 1989.**

This Turbo Pascal reference includes a good introductory chapter on object-oriented programming, Turbo Pascal-style.

Rumelhart, David, and James McClelland. *Parallel Distributed Processing.* **Cambridge, Mass.: MIT Press, 1987.**

The classic introduction and reference to the ideas and mathematics of neural networks.

Sethi, Ravi. *Programming Languages: Concepts and Constructs.* **Reading, Mass.: Addison-Wesley, 1989.**

An excellent study of the development, design, and content of modern programming languages. Contains several fine chapters on object-oriented programming and good discussions of Modula-2, C++, and Smalltalk. Chapters on encapsulation, inheritance, functional programming, and logic programming and several tough, advanced chapters on interpreters and lambda calculus. Highly recommended if you're studying the development of programming languages.

Stewart, Ian. *Does God Play Dice? The Mathematics of Chaos.* **New York, N.Y.: Basil Blackwell, 1989.**

An in-depth study of the mathematics of chaos, turbulence, and strange attractors. Combines history, mathematics, and philosophy. Good discussions of logistic mapping, Lorenz and Henon attractors, and fractals.

Vasey, Phil, et al. *Prolog++ Programming Reference Manual.* **London, England: Logic Programming Associates Ltd., 1990.**

One of those rare creatures: a programming manual that really shines. Besides showing you how to program in Prolog++, the object-oriented version of Prolog, it compares object-oriented languages and discusses the key features of OOP. Available from Quintus Computer Systems in Mountain View, Calif.

Yourdon, E.N., and L.L. Constantine. *Structured Design.* **Englewood Cliffs, N.J.: Prentice-Hall, 1979.**

A classic work on structured methodology by the gurus of the field.

Zinc Interface Library Programmer's Guide. **Pleasant Grove, Utah: Zinc Software Inc., 1990.**

An excellent OOP-style discussion (and implementation) of event-driven software, part of a two-volume manual that accompanies the Zinc Interface Library for C++. Zinc has implemented a good event-driven interface that you can use to derive more elaborate interfaces.

I also recommend the following software package:

NeuroSym Neurocomputing Library. Houston, Texas: NeuroSym Corp., 1990.

The most complete C library of neural networks I know of. Includes a dozen neural networks (back-propagating; self-organizing, etc.) that you can call from your C code. An object-oriented version is in the works.

A Concise Comparison of C++, Turbo Pascal, and Smalltalk

C++

C++ was developed by Bjarne Stroustrup at AT&T Bell Laboratories. It's a strongly typed hybrid object-oriented language that gives you the option of using user-defined types (classes) as well as functions and ordinary data structures. It includes the three key features of object-oriented programming — encapsulation, inheritance, and polymorphism — and allows multiple inheritance (a descendant can have more than one immediate ancestor) and operator overloading (any operator can have new functionality within any user-defined type). It also specifies a pure abstract method.

In addition, C++ lets you implement methods in-line, thus avoiding the overhead of a function call. In-line methods replace parameterized macros, as follows:

```
class WithInLine {
    int a;
public:
    void AMethod() { a = 0; }      // in-line
};
```

C++ constructors and destructors share the type name:

```
class AnyClass {
public:
    AnyClass();               // constructor
    ~AnyClass();              // destructor
};
```

Constructors and destructors can be called automatically (by default) by the compiler. (See the glossary for more information.)

In C++, any method declared as virtual remains virtual through all derived classes.

Turbo Pascal

Turbo Pascal is another strongly typed hybrid object-oriented language incorporating both object-oriented techniques and traditional structured techniques. You have the option of using user-defined types (objects) in a hybrid language, but you can still use functions and ordinary data structures.

Although Turbo Pascal implements the key features of object-oriented programming, it doesn't have all the features of C++. In particular, it only allows single inheritance (a descendant type can have only one immediate ancestor) and has a different approach for limiting access to its members from outside an object type.

Turbo Pascal only allows data encapsulation to be enforced using the keyword *private*, limiting access to objects, functions, and procedures declared within the same unit.

Constructors and destructors can be any unused legal name and must be explicitly called:

```
AnyObject = object
    constructor Init;              { constructor }
    destructor CleanUp;            { destructor }
end;
```

In Turbo Pascal, any method declared as virtual must be declared virtual in all subsequent derived objects:

```
BaseObject = object
    constructor Setup;
    procedure AMethod; virtual;
    destructor Finish;
end;
```

```
Derived = object (BaseObject)
  constructor Setup;
  procedure AMethod; virtual;
  destructor Finish;
end;
```

In Turbo Pascal, as in C++, memory management is left to the user.

Smalltalk

Smalltalk, the granddaddy of object-oriented languages and descendant of Simula-67, was developed at Xerox's Palo Alto Research Center. Because this language effectively treats everything in its system as an object, it's sometimes called a *pure* object-oriented language.

The Smalltalk environment usually features editing, windowing, menuing, mouse handling, and browsing. It exhibits the key features of object-oriented languages, and every object in the Smalltalk system inherits from the root object.

Like other object-oriented languages, Smalltalk distinguishes between objects and classes. An object is an instance of a class. All instance variables of a Smalltalk class are by default private to that object; thus, it strongly enforces data encapsulation. It also includes a built-in memory management system, sometimes known as *garbage collection.*

Several other languages also have object-oriented features: Actor (OOP for Windows), Objective-C (a portable, Smalltalk-like syntax added to C), and Eiffel (a software-engineering language described in Bertrand Meyer's *Object-oriented Software Construction*).

Index

A

Actor 20, 26
Algol 31
ANSI C 10, 19
ANSI C++ 11, 19
artificial intelligence 140
   and OOP 142, 153
attractors 90
   Henon 98
   in state space 87
   mathematic 91
   strange 81, 92, 98
   wild 98

B

behaviors and characteristics 21, 25, 26, 30, 33, 44, 73
   and abstract types 123
   in expert systems 149
Betz, David 142
binding
   dynamic/late 6, 7, 36, 37, 66
   early/static 6, 36, 37, 66

C

C++ vs. Turbo Pascal 10, 11, 40
Cain, Ron 218
chaos 81, 90
class 21
   access 40, 41
   declaring 22
   defining 22
   implementing 45
   vs. *struct* 148

CLOS 142
composition 26, 58, 95
constructors 11, 37, 38, 45-49, 118
Cox, Brad 70

D

Data structures 19
   record in Turbo Pascal 21, 22, 23, 79, 138
   struct in C++ 21, 22, 23, 79, 138
delete in C++ 118, 137
design (OOP) 12, 13, 18, 53, 54, 79, 191-215
   and polymorphism 116
   for change 152-153
   guidelines 198, 199
   object 202, 203
   structured 191-197
destructors 38, 45-48, 118
dispose in Turbo Pascal 118, 137
dynamic
   debugging 125
   memory allocation 38
   objects 48, 125
   processes 17, 18, 49
   style 38
   variables 138

E

Eiffel 20, 26
encapsulation 21, 23, 24, 51, 70
expert systems 140-141
   vs. neural networks 168

F

Flavors 142
Forth 8
Fogg, Larry 196
fractal nature 93
friend 41

G

GUI and OOP 211, 218

H

hierarchy 63, 64, 80
    and extension 85
    and programs 127
hybrid languages 3, 8, 9, 10, 20, 31, 36

I

imperative languages 74
inheritance 5, 7, 24, 26, 27, 28, 29, 30,
31, 32, 34, 36, 51, 58, 73, 76
    and attractors 93
    multiple 26, 27, 28, 31
in-line 83
instances (of types) 19, 26, 43, 45, 50, 61,
66, 141
    and linked lists 119
    and memory allocation 117
    of polymorphic types 137
    = variable 44

K

Koenig, Andrew 14

L

language extensibility 8
linked lists 119-124, 140
LISP 73, 142
Loops 142

M

members in C++ 19
memory allocation/deallocation 117-119

messages 4, 6, 20, 25, 32, 34, 35, 39, 42,
49-51, 78
    and polymorphism 111, 116, 122, 125
    correct performance of 70, 118
    general 112
    to constructors 118
methods 19, 25, 32, 35, 63
    virtual 7, 36, 37, 48, 85, 124, 149
modeling 17, 61, 80
    and computers 165
    and neural networks 168
    and OOP 89
    as black art 86
    composed 95
    state 94
    = state generator 97
Modula-2 39

N

neural networks 165-190
    and messages 166-168
    and objects 169
    as a dynamic system 166
    deriving 176
    vs. expert systems 168
new 116, 117, 137

O

Object Management Group 219, 223
object types 19, 21, 23, 24, 27, 28, 30, 32,
42, 51, 64
    declaring 22
    defining 22, 68
    discovering 95, 178, 202, 204-210
    dynamic evolution of 69
    extending the language 70
    finding 165, 169
    implementing 45
    initializing 37
    rules for creating 62
Objective-C 26, 70
objects 4, 21, 24, 26, 32, 38, 70

as programs 39
assembling 203
finding 143, 202, 204-210
in a dynamic world 49
thinking in 54-60
vs. units/modules 53
operator overloading in C++ 60
overhead/inefficiency 7, 36

P

PL/I 31
pointers 23, 38
tracing 125-126
VMT in Turbo Pascal 6, 11, 48, 118
VPTR in C++ 6, 11, 118
polymorphic types 137
polymorphism 30, 32, 33, 34, 35, 51, 75, 111, 113
Presentation Manager and OOP 211
private 40, 41, 48
procedural languages/programming 3, 5, 7, 8, 12, 14, 20, 42, 49, 50, 70, 195
Prolog++ 73, 74, 142
protected 40, 41
protocol/interface 34, 62, 68, 80, 116
public 22, 23, 40, 41
pure languages 20

R

reusable code/objects 7, 8, 30, 67, 68, 70
extending systems 100, 203
extensible libraries 80, 212, 220

S

scope 24
Simula 4, 31
simulate 4, 17, 53, 58, 81
Smalltalk 8, 9, 15, 20, 26, 31, 223
Stroustrup, Bjarne 11
structured languages/programming 18, 20, 31, 99, 214, 217

T

Tao 3, 12, 13, 17, 20, 28, 37, 38, 49, 53, 73, 111, 137, 155, 191, 217
Turbo Pascal vs. C++ 10, 11, 40
types 3, 4, 13, 42-45
abstract 33, 34, 42, 58, 63, 66, 67, 68, 69, 82, 123
base 4, 5, 24, 29, 30, 31, 32, 34, 37, 63, 66, 67, 76, 78
as check 120
built-in 8, 9, 25, 39, 42, 43, 45, 60
checking 6, 11
concrete 67, 68
derived 4, 5, 7, 24, 25, 29, 30, 32, 34, 35, 37, 61, 67, 78
finding 165
general 73, 74
generic 34, 35
hierarchy 5
not individuals 61
object 19, 21, 23, 24, 27, 28, 30, 32, 37, 40, 42, 45, 51, 64, 68
polymorphic 137
predefined 70
specific 73
subtypes 5, 61, 74, 82
user-defined 3, 9, 12, 19, 23, 25, 38, 40, 44, 45, 53, 117

V

virtual 7, 36, 37, 48, 66, 68, 69, 85
behaviors 112
methods 124, 149
VMT in Turbo Pascal 118
VTABLE in C++ 118

W

Windows and OOP 211, 218

X

XLisp 142

A Library of Technical References from M&T Books

NetWare User's Guide
by Edward Liebing

Endorsed by Novell, this book informs NetWare users of the services and utilities available, and how to effectively put them to use. Contained is a complete task-oriented reference that introduces users to NetWare and guides them through the basics of NetWare menu-driven utilities and command line utilities. Each utility is illustrated, thus providing a visual frame of reference. You will find general information about the utilities, then specific procedures to perform the task in mind. Utilities discussed include NetWare v2.1 through v2.15. For advanced users, a workstation troubleshooting section is included, describing the errors that occur. Two appendixes, describing briefly the services available in each NetWare menu or command line utility are also included.

Book only	Item #071-0	$24.95

Blueprint of a LAN
by Craig Chaiken

Blueprint of a LAN provides a hands-on introduction to microcomputer networks. For programmers, numerous valuable programming techniques are detailed. Network administrators will learn how to build and install LAN communication cables, configure and troubleshoot network hardware and software, and provide continuing support to users. Included are a very inexpensive zero-slot, star topology network, remote printer and file sharing, remote command execution, electronic mail, parallel processing support, high-level language support, and more. Also contained is the complete Intel 8086 assembly language source code that will help you build an inexpensive to install, local area network. An optional disk containing all source code is available.

Book & Disk (MS-DOS)	Item #066-4	$39.95
Book only	Item #052-4	$29.95

LAN Troubleshooting Handbook
by Mark A. Miller

This book is specifically for users and administrators who need to identify problems and maintain a LAN that is already installed. Topics include LAN standards, the OSI model, network documentation, LAN test equipment, cable system testing, and more. Addressed are specific issues associated with troubleshooting the four most popular LAN architectures: ARCNET, Token Ring, Ethernet, and StarLAN. Each are closely examined to pinpoint the problems unique to its design and the hardware. Handy checklists to assist in solving each architecture's unique network difficulties are also included.

Book & Disk (MS-DOS)   **Item #056-7**   **$39.95**

Book only   **Item #054-0**   **$29.95**

Building Local Area Networks with Novell's NetWare
by Patrick H. Corrigan and Aisling Guy

From the basic components to complete network installation, here is the practical guide that PC system integrators will need to build and implement PC LANs in this rapidly growing market. The specifics of building and maintaining PC LANs, including hardware configurations, software development, cabling, selection criteria, installation, and on-going management are described in a clear "how-to" manner with numerous illustrations and sample LAN management forms. *Building Local Area Networks* gives particular emphasis to Novell's NetWare, Version 2.1. Additional topics covered include the OS/2 LAN manager, Tops, Banyan VINES, internetworking, host computer gateways, and multisystem networks that link PCs, Apples, and mainframes.

Book & Disk (MS-DOS)   **Item #025-7**   **$39.95**

Book only   **Item #010-9**   **$29.95**

1-800-533-4372 (in CA 1-800-356-2002)

NetWare Supervisor's Guide
by John T. McCann, Adam T. Ruef, and Steven L. Guengerich

Written for network administrators, consultants, installers, and
power users of all versions of NetWare, including NetWare 386.
Where other books provide information on using NetWare at a
workstation level, this definitive reference focuses on how to
administer NetWare. Contained are numerous examples which
include understanding and using NetWare's undocumented
commands and utilities, implementing system fault tolerant
LANs, refining installation parameters to improve network
performance, and more.

Book only   Item #111-3 $24.95

LAN Protocol Handbook
by Mark A. Miller, P.E.

Requisite reading for all network administrators and software
developers needing in-depth knowledge of the internal protocols
of the most popular network software. It illustrates the techniques of protocol analysis—the step-by-step process of unrav-
eling LAN software failures. Detailed are how Ethernet, IEEE
802.3, IEEE 802.5, and ARCNET networks transmit frames of
information between workstations. From that foundation, it
presents LAN performnce measurements, protocol analysis
methods, and protocol analyzer products. Individual chapters
thoroughly discuss Novell's NetWare, 3Com's 3+ and 3+Open,
IBM Token-Ring related protocols, and more!

Book only   Item 099-0 $34.95

1-800-533-4372 (in CA 1-800-356-2002)

NetWare Administrator's Guide
by Russell Frye

This comprehensive guide is for all NetWare administrators responsible for the daily management of a NetWare network. Through in-depth discussions and detailed explanations, administrators will learn how to increase their network's performance and simplify file server management. All utilities available from the console are thoroughly examined. Readers will learn how to link a NetWare network to other networks, set up and manage remote access services, keep track of cabling layouts, monitor network operations, manage shared resources, and much more.

Book only   **Item #125-3**   **$34.95**

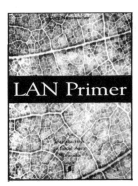

LAN Primer
An Introduction to Local Area Networks
by Greg Nunemacher

A complete introduction to local area networks (LANs), this book is a must for anyone who needs to know basic LAN principles. It includes a complete overview of LANs, clearly defining what a LAN is, the functions of a LAN, and how LANs fit into the field of telecommunications. The author discusses the specifics of building a LAN, including the required hardware and software, an overview of the types of products available, deciding what products to purchase, and assembling the pieces into a working LAN system. LAN Basics also includes case studies that illustrate how LAN principles work. Particular focus is given to ethernet and Token-Ring. Approx. 240 pp.

Book only   **Item #127-X**   **$24.95**

1-800-533-4372 (in CA 1-800-356-2002)

O R D E R   F O R M

To Order: Return this form with your payment to M&T books, 501 Galveston Drive, Redwood City, CA 94063 or **call toll-free 1-800-533-4372 (in California, call 1-800-356-2002).**

ITEM #	DESCRIPTION	DISK	PRICE

Subtotal	
CA residents add sales tax ___%	
Add $3.50 per item for shipping and handling	
TOTAL	

Charge my:

☐ **Visa**
☐ **MasterCard**
☐ **AmExpress**

☐ **Check enclosed, payable to M&T Books.**

CARD NO. _____

SIGNATURE _____ EXP. DATE _____

NAME _____

ADDRESS _____

CITY _____

STATE _____ ZIP _____

M&T GUARANTEE: If your are not satisfied with your order for any reason, return it to us within 25 days of receipt for a full refund. Note: Refunds on disks apply only when returned with book within guarantee period. Disks damaged in transit or defective will be promptly replaced, but cannot be exchanged for a disk from a different title.

7110